C0-AXE-769

WOMEN IN THE PULPIT:

Is God
an Equal Opportunity Employer?

Books by William Proctor

SURVIVAL ON THE CAMPUS: A HANDBOOK FOR
CHRISTIAN STUDENTS

HELP WANTED: FAITH REQUIRED

THE COMMUNE KIDNAPPING

WOMEN
IN THE PULPIT

Is God an Equal Opportunity Employer?

PRISCILLA and WILLIAM PROCTOR

Doubleday & Company, Inc.
Garden City, New York
1976

Library of Congress Cataloging in Publication Data
Proctor, Priscilla, 1945-
Women in the Pulpit.

1. Women clergy. I. Proctor, William, joint author.
II. Title.
BV676.P77   253'.2
ISBN 0-385-00916-X
Library of Congress Catalog Card Number 75-14838

Copyright © 1975, 1976 by WILLIAM AND PRISCILLA PROCTOR
All Rights Reserved
Printed in the United States of America
BOOK DESIGN BY BENTE HAMANN
First Edition

To our mothers,
Florence and Maud,
who first showed us
a woman's gift for faith,
hope and love

Preface

This book contains the stories of women who have sensed the call of God in their innermost beings and have responded by entering the largely uncharted territory of a man's profession, the pastoral ministry. Our focus has been on the women themselves—what they think, believe and feel—rather than on trying to fathom any abstract theological or sociological significance in their careers. The pastoral encounters and confrontations, a few of which are presented as composite accounts, reflect a new style of ministry that promises to transform the face of traditional American religion. We hope that the following pages will convey to the reader not merely an intellectual understanding of these women, but a genuine participation in the sometimes frustrating, sometimes humorous, but always adventurous quality of their lives.

Many people have given us invaluable insights into the work of female pastors, but a few have been particularly helpful in directing us to sources of information. We want to thank Arabella Meadows-Rogers for her practical and scholarly advice; Brinton Lykes and Charlotte O'Neal for their gracious help with interview sources; and Eve Roshevsky and Alex Liepa for their valuable assistance as editors.

Contents

CHAPTER ONE: Not Peace, but a Sword   1

CHAPTER TWO: Is God an Equal Opportunity
Employer?   23

CHAPTER THREE: "Our Mother Who Art in
Heaven . . ."   41

CHAPTER FOUR: The Pastor's Husband   55

CHAPTER FIVE: The Masculine Mystique of
the Pulpit   71

CHAPTER SIX: The Open Woman   95

CHAPTER SEVEN: The Spiritual Specialists   117

CHAPTER EIGHT: A Foot in the Synagogue
Door   131

CHAPTER NINE: Rumblings in the Roman
Church   147

CHAPTER TEN: Filled with the Spirit   165

WOMEN IN THE PULPIT:

*Is God
an Equal Opportunity Employer?*

CHAPTER ONE

Not Peace, but a Sword

Riverside Church, on New York City's Upper West Side, has a stately, awe-inspiring sanctuary. The Gothic ceilings which seem to stretch up to the heavens and the shadowy, cavernous recesses behind the enormous pillars imbue the visitor with a sense of his own insignificance, a sense of the pregnant presence of God. Riverside is usually a house of worship, a house of prayer. But on a cold winter day in January 1974, it became the scene of angry, hateful words—and bloodletting.

The Archbishop of Canterbury was visiting the city and had been asked to attend a series of services sponsored at Riverside by the Episcopal Church's conservative Trinity Institute. The program seemed sedate enough, except for one thing: the movement to ordain women as priests had been gaining momentum at about this time among Episcopalians. Such a large gathering of prominent Anglicans and Episcopalians was the ideal audience to confront with the gripes and demands of the women. One of the denomination's more outspoken female deacons, twenty-eight-year-old Carter Heyward, decided to lead a demonstration outside Riverside to point up what she considered the discriminatory policies of the church against women.

"It was an all-male show over there at Riverside, and we decided to have a quiet, dignified march to protest," Carter said. "We wore armbands and handed out flyers to those attending the services as a witness for all women in all churches."

Carter had every reason to assume that the reaction to her protest would be subdued—until she helped two bishops serve Communion the next day in the Riverside sanctuary. She and Carol Anderson, another Episcopal deacon who was also a vocal women's ordination advocate, had been asked to participate in the service. The situation was tailor-made for trouble. Both Carter and Carol had developed reputations as impatient, aggressive women's liberationists in the church. They had joined forces only a month before at Manhattan's Church of St. John the Divine in an attempt to pressure New York Bishop Paul Moore, Jr., to ordain them at the same time he ordained several male deacons. When he refused, they staged a walkout with many of their supporters in the sanctuary, and that demonstration had left a bad taste in the mouths of many conservative Episcopalians.

The Riverside service started off serenely enough. Carter and Carol, wearing their clerical collars and robes, were stationed at different sets of steps at the front of the huge sanctuary. They held wine chalices for each of the two bishops who were serving the bread, or "body" of Christ. As long lines of communicants formed in the aisles, the bishops handed each parishioner a morsel of bread, and the two women offered a sip from the communal wine cup.

Because a large number in the congregation were ministers, Carol saw nothing remarkable about a serious-looking young Episcopal priest who walked up to receive the Eucharist in the company of an Episcopal nun in full black habit. They took the bread from Bishop Paul Moore and then reached for Carol's chalice. But as she moved the cup toward the priest's lips, his face twisted in fury. He grabbed the chalice, whipped it toward his chest, and spat out, "Go to hell!"

"I can't, I'm busy," retorted Carol, a statuesque twenty-nine-year-old redhead, as she kept a firm hold on the cup.

"I've learned to hold onto that chalice no matter what," Carol said. "I didn't let go, and we just stood there, tugging at one another."

The priest seemed rather stunned by Carol's quick response and her refusal to give up the wine cup, but the nun behind him lost no time in taking the offensive. She stuck her nose in Carol's face and rasped menacingly, "You're ruining the church! You go to hell!"

Before Carol could respond again, the two moved on, and the line of communicants resumed their calm, usually orderly Communion ceremony. The entire incident had happened so fast and had involved such a quiet—though vicious—exchange that apparently no one else—not even the bishop, who was standing a few feet away—had heard anything.

As Carol was engaging in this wrestling match, the sandy-haired, animated Carter was facing similar opposition on the far side of the church. A young priest, just as serious and austere-looking as the one who had confronted Carol, drank the wine as Carter held it for him. But instead of letting go of the cup, he dug his long fingernails deeper and deeper into the woman deacon's hand. As the searing pain shot up into her wrist, the priest said under his breath, "I hope you burn in hell!"

But Carter refused to drop the cup or discontinue her part of the service, as he apparently hoped she would. She gritted her teeth and jerked the cup away from him. After a brief struggle, he let go and hurriedly, with eyes cast down, left the steps and was lost in the crowd.

"I'll never forget the way he looked at me before he walked away. If looks could kill, I'd be dead now," Carter shuddered afterward.

As the next person came up for the wine, she glanced at her hand and saw three maroon claw marks and drops of blood trickling down her hand.

"I was stunned," she said. "It was like a state of amnesia setting in. All I remember for the last half hour of that service was wiping the blood off my hand. At the end of the service, still feeling numb, I walked over to my office at Union Seminary, sat down and just stared at my hand. It was still bleeding. I fell apart at that point."

She couldn't keep the tears back now, and she began to shake all over. She had to talk to somebody. The president of Union and his wife were the first ones who came to mind, so she rushed to their home and "fell all to pieces."

After this experience, Carter Heyward's path was fixed. For her, it would be full ordination, or nothing. She eventually chose to defy the religious establishment and be ordained illegally with ten other women in Philadelphia in the summer of 1974. But Carol Anderson, whose experience at Riverside was similar and whose support of

women's rights in the Episcopal Church had been at least as strong as
Carter's, chose a different route. Though offered the chance to be ordained irregularly with the others, she elected to obey church policies
that opposed women's ordination. Why should two young women
who were alike in so many ways choose such different paths? The answer to this question is rooted in an understanding of the traumatic
choices that Carter, Carol and most other contemporary women
ministers have had to make as they have sorted out their conflicting
calls to serve the needs of God, their fellow believers and themselves.

When Carol Anderson left her native New Jersey to attend college
in Pennsylvania, she was well on her way toward becoming a naïve
humanist who believed that all the wrongs in the world could be
cured by bringing out the basic goodness in every human being. But
then she went down to South Carolina as an exchange student at a
small black college, and her outspokenness on the virtues of civil
rights got her beaten up quite severely by some rednecks one bright
Easter morning.

"This was the first time I had come into contact with raw evil, and
the hate I saw was so deep and strong that I couldn't fit it into my
philosophy about the basic goodness of man," she said. "I decided
that religion might have the answer I was looking for, so I decided to
major in religion after returning from the South."

But the abstract intellectual slant of her religious studies didn't satisfy her, nor did most of the diluted, half-baked religious commitment
she found on her nominally Methodist college campus. Then she met
two Episcopal priests, the first Christians she had known who took
"social action and religious commitment seriously." One had gone to
the Episcopal Theological School in Cambridge, Massachusetts, so
Carol decided to apply there too.

Impressed with the serious Christians she found at seminary, she
was confirmed in the Episcopal Church and soon decided that her
desire to help people in the community could best be satisfied by
going into the parish ministry. As she worked through the relationship between her new Christian faith and her commitment to
social action, Carol also began to develop a contemplative side to her
nature that she had never known before.

"I've started to think deeply about the personal nature of what I call God," she explained. "I found in college that my human experience by itself didn't provide me with an adequate understanding of life. The Christian story does give me that kind of understanding. I used to think my own experience was pretty ultimate. But I've finally realized the truth of what a college professor said to me one time: 'Those feelings you have in you may be revelation—but they may also be constipation!' I've become a theist in the last few years. I've come to believe God is something other than my own existence and that God was in Christ, reconciling the world to himself in some unique way."

While in seminary, Carol found during her practical training in local churches that the parish ministry offered opportunities to combine her blossoming Christian consciousness with her basic need to help others. She was aware that women could not be ordained as priests in the Episcopal Church, and she also knew that only a priest could serve as a rector, or the head pastor of a church. But despite these roadblocks that threatened to keep her from realizing her full potential within the Episcopal hierarchy, she decided to be ordained as an Episcopal deacon and look for a job in an urban parish.

Although Carol was a latecomer to the Episcopal tradition, Carter Heyward was an Episcopalian "almost from birth." Her parents— a "typically Southern churchgoing family"—joined the Episcopal Church in Hendersonville, North Carolina, when she was three years old.

"I was always active in the church," she said. "As a child, I loved it. Part of it was that I liked being alone. I was an only child until I was six, and I spent a lot of time outdoors with animals. Church was an extension of that way of life. I could go into the sanctuary and sit quietly and nobody would bother me."

It was during this early period that she started having fantasies about being a priest. "I saw myself up there leading the services. I didn't think of myself as a female as much as a *person* at that time. I grew up without any kind of role definition as to what little girls do and what little boys do. I could as easily imagine myself as a cowboy as a cowgirl. I played with trucks as well as with dolls. I climbed trees, and then dressed up like a little girl to go to church. I was a pretty androgynous kid."

Carter began to lose this androgynous concept of herself as she approached adolescence, but she still found she relied on the church "as a refuge as much as anything else. I couldn't stand all of the roles that were imposed on young teen-age girls—having to dress a certain way, look a certain way, conform to what a cute, bouncy little girl should be. At first, I wanted to make it on those standards. I wanted to be a cheerleader, but I tried out and lost. There was another side of my personality that made me want to withdraw. Finally, I literally ran to the church, full speed ahead—into church groups and worship and everything, looking for a way out of this social mirage way out there that kept beckoning, but then eluding me."

The church was a place where Carter could be herself, where she could let her hair down. Still in the last days of childhood, sensing what she was about to say was impossible but not yet knowing exactly why, twelve-year-old Carter revealed to her father those deep-rooted feelings, that sense of call that had been gnawing at her for years.

"Daddy, I know what I'm going to be—I'm going to be a priest," she said. "God's calling me to be a priest."

Her father didn't know what to do with that statement but she knows it made him "very sad." Then as the realities of the world overcame her as a teen-ager, she altered her ambition: she decided to become a nun. For two years, she and two of her friends planned to enter an Episcopal female order. Gradually, as she got older and entered Randolph-Macon Woman's College in Virginia, she lost all interest in being a full-time religious. But she majored in religion and a sense of spiritual call still smoldered deep inside her when she finally decided to enter Union Theological Seminary in New York City and teach religion.

"All hell broke loose inside of me during my first year at Union in 1967," she said with a trace of a Southern drawl. "Part of that emotional turmoil had to do with the gross difference between my realistic occupational expectations and these deep yearnings I had to be a priest. It was that year that I began to get back in touch with being ordained, even though I didn't know how to go about it."

The groundwork for part of her vocational interest was laid by the Episcopal Church itself. Carter was allowed to do field work in a Bronx parish, and she immediately knew she belonged in that sort of ministry—but how to get into it remained the primary question.

"It was all so funny and uncomfortable," she said. "It didn't make any sense that I was there preaching and counseling since I couldn't be a priest and go into that kind of work. Yet there were men working right next to me who could be priests."

At the same time that Carter was facing this occupational crisis, she was also trying to sort out a variety of personal problems—"relationships to men, to women, to authority—the whole thing about whether there was a God, the anti-war movement. It was an emotional and chaotic year for me."

To top it all off, she fell in love with an Anglican priest working in Charlotte, North Carolina. Her relationship with him, coupled with all her other problems, induced her to leave seminary and work in a North Carolina parish for eighteen months as a parish assistant.

"The romantic interest brought me down there, and I also wanted to get out of the vocational pressure cooker in New York City, so I just split," she recalls. "That was the most formidable period in my growing up. I worked full time in that parish and did everything but perform the sacraments. And as I began to examine my relationship with this man, I saw I was the one who would have to make the decision about us. I had to decide either for him, or for my own career."

Because of the thoroughly positive experience she had in that Southern parish, romance lost out and the relationship came to an end. "People in that church had responded to me well, and I responded well to the work. I wanted to learn more and do more. I was very good at that kind of work, as good as I'd ever been at anything. I found people didn't mind my being a woman; in fact, some people were drawn to me for that reason."

When Carter returned to Union in 1970, she was quite confident in her abilities as a professional church person. She started seeing a therapist and attending a consciousness-raising group with other female seminary students, and many of the problems which had seemed insoluble before now became quite manageable. Although she didn't know what to do about ordination at first, the Episcopal Church ironically soon provided her with a plan of action by opening up its order of deacons to women on the same basis as men. Carter, now a full-blown feminist, applied immediately to the North Carolina bishop for acceptance as a postulant. She says she was turned down on the ground that she was "confused."

"He didn't say what I was confused about," she said. "I might have accepted a decision like that from a high church official a couple of years before, but I wasn't about to accept his judgment at that point. So many women have been told the same thing by other bishops—that they're 'confused.' It's a good catchall word. Maybe it means we're too pushy, or that our idea of a woman's potential in the ministry is too fuzzy. In any case, the bishops don't have to account to anybody for a decision like that, so I turned to Bishop Paul Moore of New York."

As Carter recalls, Moore was positive about her application, but he was concerned that she was angry about the other bishop's rejection. "He told me to cool off for a while and come back to see him later," she said. She waited a few months and then applied and was accepted as a postulant in the spring of 1972. She was ordained a deacon in the summer of 1973. Then, armed with a degree from Union, she decided to subordinate her interest in parish work and prepared to turn the Episcopal Church and its policies on women upside down.

As Carter was pursuing a checkered, tumultuous path toward the diaconate, Carol Anderson's career pattern was considerably smoother. Having found, as did Carter, that she liked her practical seminary training in local parishes, she moved into a staff position at the St. James' Episcopal Church on Manhattan's fashionable Upper East Side. She immediately got involved in people-oriented parish work—counseling, preaching, funerals and baptisms. As a deacon, she could not give blessings and absolutions or consecrate the bread and wine during Communion; and she was barred from serving as rector of a parish. Only a fully ordained priest could perform those functions.

But in the sphere in which she could operate, Carol quickly found that she could hardly wait to get up at seven o'clock every morning and was reluctant to go to bed at midnight.

"I really do enjoy the parish ministry," Carol says emphatically. "And I do seem to have some advantages being a woman. When people are sick in the hospital, for example, they seem to have a need to be mothered. In this type of ministry, I've found some patients identify with me more easily than they do with a man because of this mother thing. Or when I'm doing a funeral, a member of the grieving family might say, 'Gee, it's good to have someone like you to talk to—it's nice to have a woman because women are more understanding in situations like this.'"

Carol soon found after she embarked on her parish ministry that "women are freer than men to show they care through words, touch, feeling. I think my whole approach to preaching and worship is more experimental than the guys'. I can express myself more easily through feminine kinds of life experiences."

One Sunday, for example, she was assigned to conduct a baptism ceremony at the main morning service. She had a very warm feeling toward the baby and cradled it and cuddled it in front of the congregation as a mother might hold her own child. It was as though a Raphael madonna had briefly come to life at this staid Manhattan church. At the end of the service, she kissed the baby tenderly and said, "Welcome as the newest member of St. James' Parish."

Then Carol handed the baby back to the parents, and turned toward the front of the church as a signal to her fellow pastor that the rest of the service could continue. But she saw that the priest was crying.

"The symbol of you as a woman, and the motherly image of you with this baby in your arms—it was so beautiful I was moved to tears," he told her later.

Carol had been unaware of the impact she was having, but she suddenly realized how significant her role in that baptism had been. "The baptism rite has been around for two thousand years, but there are so few people who have ever understood that a person can be both a minister and a mother in the role I performed that morning," she said. "I was doing the sacrament of the church with authority because I was ordained as a deacon to do it. And at the same time I was performing a distinctively motherly function."

But not all of Carol's experiences at St. James have been so positive. When she first started work at the three-thousand-member, sophisticated urban church, she noticed a "sort of back-off-and-let's-see-what-happens" attitude. A number of people were uncomfortable with the idea of having a woman minister, but they were not so crass as to come right out and say so. Instead, several parishioners, all women, took an indirect approach: they let it be known they didn't approve of Carol's practice of wearing earrings during Communion service.

"The women just couldn't take those damned earrings," Carol said with a grin. "The men didn't care, though. They thought it was great."

The earring criticism soon subsided as they got used to her and saw that she wasn't interested in staging women's lib demonstrations in the sanctuary. The next step Carol noticed in her growing acceptance by the congregation was a sense of pride that St. James was one of the few Episcopal parishes to have a "lady minister."

"I'd get dragged around to meet visiting friends and relatives, and I was always introduced as 'our lady minister,'" Carol said dryly.

In other words, the church members had mostly started to accept her, but primarily as an oddity—a "lady minister" rather than just a "minister." She found that people "will come listen to a woman because a woman is different. It's like having a famous person there. They pay more attention when I preach, and I'm almost always told I do a good job. They think I'm fantastic. Part of that may be my skill, but not all of it. People just don't expect a woman to do as well as a man, and they're pleasantly surprised when I do."

To show that these attitudes are deeply ingrained, Carol is fond of quoting an eighteenth-century authority, Boswell's *Life of Dr. Johnson*: "Sir, a woman preaching is like a dog's walking on his hind legs. It is not done well; but you are surprised to find it done at all."

Almost imperceptibly, the sense of novelty about Carol wore off, and one Sunday after she had been at St. James for a couple of years she noticed that nearly everyone was referring to her just as "our minister."

"I almost cried," she said. "And it wasn't that I had become one of the boys." Instead, she realized she had finally been accepted as an ordinary, competent minister, rather than a spiritual freak.

As Carol underwent the process of adjustment at St. James, some of the toughest problems she faced revolved around her status as a single woman. For one thing, there was the perennial problem of flirtation and seduction at cocktail parties.

"I've been to a number of parties with parishioners where there's been a lot of heavy drinking," she said. "I'm sometimes the target of seduction language in situations like that. There seems to be a feeling on the part of many men that there's got to be a woman under all that Sunday clerical garb."

In the midst of the double entendres and suggestive comments, Carol's sense of humor induces her to "play with them a little bit, though it never comes to anything. The woman minister has to be secure and careful about her own needs to be sure she keeps things under control."

But despite Carol's best efforts, the men sometimes feel embarrassed after they sober up and realize what they've said to their woman minister. On one occasion, an elderly but quite handsome fellow had several stiff drinks and began to roll his eyes and smile romantically at the smooth-complexioned, open-faced Carol.

"He came over and put his arm around me and bussed me a couple of times," she explained with a laugh. "I played the game with him for a while, partly because I didn't want to embarrass him and partly because I like to do that sort of thing. It's innocent enough."

But this amorous gentleman seemed a little uncomfortable when Carol saw him the next Sunday in the church vestibule after services. He hung back and avoided her, as though he was not sure what her reaction to him had been. To put him at ease, Carol swept back her long reddish hair, smiled broadly at him and said, "Hey, right here," as she pointed toward her cheek. He gave her a quick peck, and their relationship was on an even keel again.

Not all of Carol's problems as a single woman have been resolved so simply, however. "There were titters when I first came here that I was a lesbian," she said wryly. "I suppose that's a charge that many aggressive single women face."

Several married women in the parish came to her rescue when such accusations were raised behind Carol's back. "Hell, no! She'd just as soon have someone in bed with her that's male!" one female defender said on overhearing such gossip.

"I suppose as far as they were concerned that was better than being a lesbian," Carol said, "but I hope that didn't give them the idea I was promiscuous with men."

On one occasion, a strange woman confronted Carol directly after a church service: "You're a lesbian!" the woman screamed. "I know all about you!"

Carol was stunned speechless for a moment by the fervor of the attack, but a small, elderly woman intervened: "She is not a lesbian!" the woman countered, jutting her jaw toward the offender. "I know she has a boy friend!"

Carol said later she thought her defender was "kind of cute," but she realized how deep the feelings of some church people run on the homosexual issue. "I've been approached by homosexual women, and I know a number of ordained women ministers who are gay," she said. "I'm not, and most people know I'm not. I've dealt with the issue on a personal level by letting people know I'm not, though I feel if a woman is a lesbian, that's all right. They're not man-haters, for the most part. That's a label that's been used unfairly. There is a radical fringe that are man-haters, but most of those people are church-haters too. The attack on women's ordination is not too outspoken on the lesbian issue because some of the opposition to our being ordained comes from homosexual men, homosexual clergy. They're not about to rattle our cages because they know they'll get theirs rattled right back."

A more conventional problem that Carol has faced as she has become immersed in her pastoral duties is the pressure to get married. But when she tried to share this concern in a talk to her parishioners one evening at a church dinner, she was "totally misunderstood," because she quipped, "What I really need is a wife."

One traditional, conservative group came up to her after she had finished and asked with concern, "Are you gay?" A couple of militant feminists, on the other hand, criticized her for tossing around veiled sexist comments.

"What I was really saying by that comment was that a lot of entertaining goes with this job," Carol explained to them. "The fellows on the staff have wives who do those kinds of things. The men can tell their wives, 'We're having a dinner party tonight,' and then they don't have to worry about it any more. But I have to go home and cook a meal. It becomes a real problem, running around, being not only a minister but the head of a household. It gets to be a real rush. And then there are social events too—going to parties like this one. I'm a social animal in this job, and it would be nice to have a regular companion with me."

Her parishioners seemed to understand this explanation, but one thing Carol didn't tell them at that dinner was that she feels a "tremendous and deep loneliness about the whole profession of the ministry. My fantasy about marriage is that I'd find it helpful to have someone else to talk to after work, to say, 'Here's what happened today.'"

Carol's entire life has become wrapped up in the pastoral parish ministry, as she performs baptisms and funeral services, preaches and interacts on the most intimate personal levels with her parishioners. But she still has found time to participate in the women's ordination movement in the Episcopal Church, and it's at this point that her career and that of Carter Heyward coincided for a time.

One of the most important early events they participated in together was the General Convention of the Episcopal Church in Louisville, Kentucky, in the summer of 1973. They met many women there who later became their colleagues in the women's movement in the church. But the immediate goals which they lobbied for at the convention failed. Carter said she was "appalled" when the convention delegates voted down a resolution that would have enabled women to be ordained priests.

"The delegates were ninety per cent men, and they voted on the issue in a very crass way, almost as though they were deciding whether they would have roast beef or lamb for dinner. They kind of decided offhandedly that women couldn't be priests because they weren't ready for us yet. It was infuriating! Just outrageous! We were sitting up there in the balconies, and except for a very few women deputies, we weren't even allowed on the floor. I had the feeling I had gone to my own trial, and even though I'd done nothing wrong, they were finding me guilty.

"They expected us to sit there quietly and smile and act like ladies, no matter what happened. We were fairly polite, but we had a lot of time afterward to commiserate. We got angry and cursed and freaked out together. Every woman there seemed to be equally appalled. It was the ultimate dehumanizing experience. I know now what it must be like for black people to undergo the same thing, to be told they can't sit in the front of the bus. There's no way to articulate the horror I felt. I sensed this horror throughout my being when the same thing had happened to the blacks in the early sixties, but this time it was so much more personal. This time it was me and my sisters. I couldn't believe we had church leaders making these poor judgments, doing *themselves* in, as well as us. I left that convention with a God-forgive-them-because-they-don't-know-what-they're-doing kind of feeling."

When Carol and Carter returned from the convention, they immediately resolved with several other female deacons to work together toward their ordination as priests. Their first move was to set up a meeting in New York City with nine women deacons and five of the most powerful eastern bishops in the church. According to Carter, some of the dialogue in that heated confrontation in the fall of 1973 went like this:

WOMEN DEACONS: We'll get right to the point. We want to be ordained, even if it's not by a regular procedure.

BISHOPS: We'll have to think about it.

WOMEN: It's important to act quickly.

BISHOPS: We can't just go off and ordain people on our own. We'll have to check with the other bishops. We need their advice.

WOMEN: No! We have the five strongest bishops right here!

BISHOPS: This sort of thing takes months if not years to work out.

WOMEN: It's clear to us you don't see the women's situation the same way you see other minority problems. You went out on a limb for blacks. But you seem to think we're out there raising hell just because we love it!

The argument grew more and more fiery until the nine women stamped out of the room in a huff. "We walked out feeling really angry at them," Carter recalls. "Our problem has always been that the bishops and other leaders of the Episcopal Church seem to think we're talking about Tinker Toys when we talk about women."

Carter, Carol and three of the other women deacons decided at that point that some public witness to their predicament was necessary. They chose an ordination ceremony that was scheduled to be performed several weeks later at Manhattan's Church of St. John the Divine by Bishop Paul Moore. Besides feeling some public statement should be made, Carter hoped that Bishop Moore's mind might be changed and he might even ordain them during the ceremony. But the bishop found out about the demonstration several days beforehand and called Carter into his office.

"We're going to do it," she warned resolutely, but would not tell him what the women were planning to say.

"When we walked into that church it almost seemed as though everything was surrealistic," Carter remembered. "It was a scene that bordered between drama and reality. Everything seemed to be staged. There were even chairs waiting for us at a designated spot in the church."

As the ceremony proceeded, Bishop Moore announced, "If anyone knows any reason why this ordination should not proceed, let him come forward."

Because the women had been unable to get a male priest to give an address for them, Carter stood up and said, "Of course there are reasons why this ordination shouldn't proceed! Injustice is being perpetrated at this ordination because there are ten deacons who should be ordained here, five men and five women, and the five women apparently won't be ordained. Therefore, the ordination shouldn't go forward. We don't come to block the ordination, but to join it. If we're not ordained, then peace in the house of bishops obviously means more than justice. The law of man means more than the law of God."

At the end of the ceremony, the women kneeled at the bishop's feet as he began to lay his hands on the men's heads and completed their ordination. When he got to the women, he merely said, "Bless you, my sisters. Go in peace."

Instead of waiting for the end of the service, the women stood up and walked out of the church and were followed by a large contingent of their supporters. The "passing of the peace," where the members of the congregation give one another a Christian greeting, was just beginning in the service.

As Carter explained their action, "We felt that if he didn't ordain us, we shouldn't stay. It would have been ridiculous to stay for the passing of the peace—'peace, peace where there is no peace,' to quote Jeremiah [Jeremiah 6:14]. We weren't going to subject ourselves to that kind of brutality. Besides, it would have been impossible for us to stay because we all got to the back of the cathedral and burst into tears. It was a real scene for about a half hour. There was no way we could have stayed in that service without being torn apart, without becoming babbling, crying idiots."

Then they calmed down and returned to Union Seminary for an agape meal of wine, cheese and bread.

After this confrontation, opposition to the women escalated. The physical attacks and verbal abuse against Carter and Carol occurred the next month in the Riverside sanctuary, and the two of them seemed to be moving inseparably toward an ultimate showdown with the Episcopal Church on the ordination issue. A number of public debates on the subject of ordination were scheduled between Carter, Carol and several male priests who opposed the ordination of women priests.

Then the time came for Carter and Carol to make the most critical choice of their careers: should they risk being suspended as deacons by trying to become priests through an irregular ordination ceremony?

A number of other Episcopal women had been working out the details for just such an ordination. In June of 1974, Carter got a call while she was attending a conference in Big Sur, California.

"Carter?" a woman deacon on the other end of the line said. "Three bishops have decided to go ahead and ordain us. Would you like to attend a meeting about this in July?"

"You'd better believe I'll be there!" Carter replied.

"Okay, just keep it quiet for now."

Carol got a similar call, but instead of being enthusiastic, as she had once thought she would be, the idea of an illegal ordination caused her to experience a "mild panic."

"I'll think about it," she finally replied, and feeling quite depressed, she hung up the phone. She had been working toward the ordination of women since the late 1960s. After three years as a deacon, she wanted desperately to become a priest so that she could consummate her work in the parish ministry.

"But the possibility really scared me," she said. "I went through a real sorting-out process. I knew what Carter and the others planned to do was necessary. Otherwise, the church would never get off dead center, never break the log jam that kept women from moving forward. The priesthood of women had to be affirmed, even if the formal church wouldn't do it. The church that was emerging in the midst of the traditional, institutional church had to affirm this principle."

Carol's problem—a problem that Carter didn't face because she was only peripherally involved in parish work—was this: should she jeopardize the pastoral ministry she had worked so hard to build up in order to claim the higher, priestly ordination she felt deeply she deserved?

"I agonized for a long time," she said. "I think some of the hesitation I felt was over security. For the first time—after being a student without any money for such a long time—I had a very good job, a neat apartment. I asked myself, 'Is that the only reason you're hesitating, because you're secure?' Then I thought, 'So what if it is—is that so bad?' The voices went back and forth in my mind. I finally realized I'd probably be feeling the same reservations even if I weren't in the parish ministry at St. James, but I didn't know exactly why."

Still up in the air, Carol attended a planning meeting in Philadelphia for the ordination later that summer. As she sat around talking with some of the other women deacons and with the bishops who had agreed to perform the ordination, several insights came to her. "I saw that I was the only woman in that group who was in a full-time parish ministry," she said. "Even though the language they were using rang true, it wasn't totally applicable to my situation."

One of the women said, "If we're not ordained, we'll be making peace with the oppressor!"

"I don't think the church is oppressive," Carol responded. "It's just stupid. I wouldn't give it the dignity of being oppressive. I don't think the church works at being oppressive. It just does things haphazardly most of the time."

After returning from this meeting, Carol became convinced that there was a good chance that one result of the planned ordination would be deposition or suspension for those involved. As she thought over what the other women had been saying and understood what was going on in their lives, she realized her situation was different. "I decided it would be less painful for me to remain a deacon than to be ordained a priest and lose my ministry. The possibility of losing what was really important to me—a pastoral ministry—was an almost impossible thought for me to entertain."

So Carol Anderson backed out of the planned Philadelphia ordination. "I could accept and affirm the ordination of the other women, but I couldn't do it myself."

When she told her rector about her decision, she said he "gave a sigh of relief you could hear from Cape Cod to New York." And though Carol stuck by her decision, she remained uncomfortable with it. "I wrote Bishop Paul Moore a letter afterward saying that for me to have to choose between my ministry and my sisters was a sinful choice, a choice that I didn't ever want to have to make again."

As Carol stepped reluctantly outside the mainstream of the women's ordination movement, Carter and ten other female deacons forged ahead with their plans to defy the Episcopal hierarchy. The women and their supporters converged on Philadelphia's Church of the Advocate on July 29, 1974, and four bishops, in violation of church law and tradition, conducted the controversial service.

In a triumphal procession with the applause of the audience ringing in their ears, the participants marched down the aisle. A banner, echoing Paul's statement in Galatians 3:28, was displayed at the front of the church to proclaim the battle cry of Christian feminists: "In Christ There Is Neither Male Nor Female." The four bishops were at the head of the procession and Carter and the ten other women, wearing traditional white robes and narrow red stoles, followed. The members of the congregation began to clap even louder, and the elated expression on many of their faces made tears well up in Carter's eyes.

"It was a high point for me, especially seeing those bishops walking ahead of me and knowing how much they were putting on the line for us," she said, her voice rising emotionally. "It was moving, that they'd do that for a group of women. Episcopal services are usually staid and dignified but our ordination had an almost revivalistic exuberance and joy. There was a lot of hand clapping and shouting amens, especially during Dr. Charles Willie's sermon."

Willie, a prominent Episcopal layman, said, "We believe it is a Christian duty to disobey unjust laws." As the bishops proceeded with the ceremony, the Right Reverend Daniel Corrigan of Denver asked if there were any objections to the ordination, and someone from the back of the audience of more than a thousand shouted, "Right Reverend sir!" Then five male Episcopal priests marched to the front of the church sanctuary and charged those involved in the service with ignoring their vows to uphold church traditions and regulations and with subverting God's will.

As each of these priests spoke in turn, groans and murmurs and hisses broke out in different parts of the auditorium. "The people were annoyed, no question about that," Carter said. But when the protests were finished and the service continued, she sensed that the congregation was "Spirit-filled, and buoyant. It was quite amazing. I felt God was present there, definitely, absolutely."

Toward the end of the service, the crucial moment arrived—the laying on of hands, which signified the actual ordination. As Carter knelt with the others in front of the bishops, she felt as though she was in a "stupor, a daze. Then when I had been ordained, I stood up and extended my hand and Bishop Robert DeWitt [retired bishop of Philadelphia] took my hand and looked directly into my eyes. I've always admired his kind of theology—you can tell that he has deep spiritual roots, that he's a very holy person. I remember the look in his eye, as though he was saying 'well, we did it!' It was a very holy moment."

Carter glanced at the new women priests around her and saw victory and ecstasy in their eyes. "I knew it was their moment too," she said.

From that moment, Carter, who favors high leather boots, a clerical collar and a prominent silver cross around her neck, became a national celebrity and the focal point for the women's movement in the church. She appeared on the cover of national magazines and was lauded by the press as one of the outstanding personalities of 1974. When not on the road lecturing, the new priest spent much of her time at her apartment near Union Seminary being interviewed by the press or responding to complaints or charges from opponents.

Meanwhile, trouble was brewing in the Episcopal heirarchy. The bishops declared the ordinations invalid in a resolution passed at a meeting in Chicago only two weeks after the Philadelphia event. The presiding bishop of the Episcopal Church, the Right Reverend John M. Allin, also forbade the women from acting as priests, and Carter and the others at first abided by this directive. But then the House of Bishops affirmed the ordination of women "in principle," and Carter and the others grew restless and dissatisfied. With two of the other women priests—the Reverend Alison Cheek of Washington, D. C., and the seventy-nine-year-old Reverend Jeannette Piccard of St. Paul, Minnesota—she decided to defy church leaders by celebrating a Eucharist at Manhattan's Riverside Church. The event was scheduled for October 27, 1974.

The women decided that they would retain the traditional language in the liturgy, such as "father," "man" and "mankind," because they didn't want the service to be written off as a non-Episcopal ceremony. Carter was designated as "President of the Assembly" and decided to chant the liturgy, as is sometimes the custom at a High Mass, so that even more dignity would be added to the celebration of the sacrament.

"I'd never chanted before, but I wasn't worried about it," Carter said. "I've done some singing with a guitar, and I wasn't really concerned about my voice cracking. The thing that bothered me most was the sexist language—I wasn't happy with that. But when we actually got into the service, it didn't seem to make any difference. It was as though the old forms and old substance had been transformed."

Wearing bright yellow robes emblazoned with a red cross, Carter and the other two women moved in a procession to the Riverside altar —the same altar where she had been attacked and bloodied less than a year before. The audience of 1,500 burst into applause, and Carter sensed that "the Spirit was really flowing. I don't think it would have bothered me if anything had gone wrong. If anyone had disrupted the service, I think any of the three of us could have taken over at any point. I had the same sense of elation I felt at the ordination."

But there were no disruptions. Women from a variety of denominations spoke in support of the fight that was being waged by the Episcopalian women. And in a history-making ceremony, the three irregularly ordained female priests consecrated the bread and wine. It was the first time that they had exercised their priestly functions in public. The battle lines had been drawn on the ordination issue. The inevitable result seemed to be either the hierarchy's acceptance of Carter and the other women as priests, or their expulsion or exclusion from the Episcopal Church.

The preacher at this Eucharist was Carol Anderson. Although she remained a staunch supporter of the fight for women's ordination, the split between her stance and Carter's was now complete. Carol, having found such deep personal satisfaction in her pastoral duties, had settled firmly, though somewhat uncomfortably, into the Episcopal establishment. Carter, with no firm parish base, had become the radical standard-bearer, the cutting edge of change and perhaps disruption and disunity in the church. They are heading toward the same goals, but at different speeds and with radically different impacts on their church community. If the controversial actions of Carter and her colleagues prove justified in the long run, they may shed some light on the enigmatic words Jesus uttered to his disciples in Matthew 10:34: "Do not think that I have come to bring peace on earth; I have not come to bring peace, but a sword."

The controversy in the Episcopal Church has attracted much attention in recent years because of the way the leadership of the church has resisted giving its 150 women deacons full ordination. But even though other denominations which have opened full ordination to their women may have received less publicity, they face problems that are also potentially explosive.

The numbers of women entering seminaries and turning toward the pastoral ministry have been increasing in recent years, and at this writing there are an estimated 5,000 ordained women in the country. Among the top ten Christian churches in the United States, the United Methodist Church boasts the largest number of ordained women—about 500. Second is the United Presbyterian Church with 189. Since they opened up ordination to women in 1970, the Lutheran Church in America has ordained 24 women and the American Lutheran Church 5. The 12-million-member Southern Baptist Convention, which is the largest Protestant denomination in the country, has only about 15 ordained women. By contrast, two relatively small denominations, the United Church of Christ and the American Baptist Convention, have a high proportion of women clergy: the UCC has more than 350 ordained women and the American Baptists about 150.

But many of these women who have full pastoral powers on paper are finding they cannot get satisfactory preaching jobs. The result may be resounding blasts of female frustration that could rip the harmony of these churches apart.

CHAPTER TWO

Is God
an Equal Opportunity
Employer?

Sitting on the end of a long bench in the choir, the Reverend Druecillar Fordham could feel herself being pushed slowly off the edge and toward the floor. None of the six male preachers to her right were looking toward her, but she could see, as they shifted almost imperceptibly in her direction, that they were determined to force her off the platform. Being a large woman, she braced herself and shoved right back. The slight ripple of bodies that swept down through the bench indicated that even if she hadn't gained back any lost seat space, she was still holding her own.

Reverend Fordham, a sixtyish black woman who pastors Harlem's only Southern Baptist congregation, had been asked to participate in a Good Friday service at another Harlem church. But she found when she arrived that the six male ministers who were also involved had decided to ignore her, apparently because they didn't approve of women preachers. They didn't say a word to her in the waiting room outside the sanctuary. When the time came for the procession to the front of the church, "they jumped ahead of me two-by-two, and I had to just march right on up there by myself," she said.

Each of the seven pastors was assigned to speak on one of Jesus' last seven words as he died on the cross: ". . . my God, why hast thou forsaken me?" Druecillar was given the word "why," and when she stood up to give her address, she realized that her presentation applied better to some of the male pastors on the platform with her than it did to the lay people in the pews.

She walked up to the pulpit with her long white robe trailing behind her and surveyed the congregation for a moment. Then, in a clear, decisive voice, she began her message: "In those last few moments of severe pain and suffering on the cross, Jesus cried out to his Father in heaven, 'why?' We know why Jesus died for us at Calvary, but let's apply that word 'why' to our own lives. Ask yourselves—you who claim to be Christians—why you do some of the shameful things you do. Why do you hate people? Why do you snub them? Why don't you recognize the authority of God in your lives and treat people as Jesus treated them?"

By the time she had finished, several of the heads on the bench behind her had dropped sheepishly. As she took her seat again, she heard one of the male ministers mutter, "Man, I'm glad I don't have to preach behind her!"

The physical resistance that Druecillar encountered during that Good Friday service in Harlem is symbolic of what is happening in many denominations throughout the United States. The opposition often materializes the moment that a woman reveals she has received a "call" to the ministry and continues as she tries to find a church where she can prove that her pastoral abilities are equal to those of any man. Her family members and friends may argue that she's being unrealistic or silly because only a man can really make it in the ministry. If she overcomes that opposition, she may find that prejudice against women preachers controls the thinking of church officials and congregations. Even if she becomes ordained and gets a church, resistance from the local male ministers may hinder her from operating her parish effectively. But women who find strength in the conviction that God has chosen them for pastoral work are conquering all these obstacles.

Abigail Evans, a North Dakota native with long, tumbling blond hair and creamy white skin, would probably be a shoo-in for many "women's jobs," such as a coffee-fetching secretary or a winsome receptionist. But Abigail's career took an unconventional turn when she and a friend made the casual decision to attend a Billy Graham rally in Madison Square Garden in 1956. "We went out of curiosity," she said. "I didn't have any particular feeling about Billy Graham, but he was a celebrity."

As Graham launched into his message, Abigail began to respond in a personal way to the spiritual challenge he offered. Bits and pieces of his message struck deeply into her being: "If you're going to have purpose, you have to make a decision . . . The Bible says you have to give your life totally to Christ . . . put him first so your life will have some direction . . ."

When Graham called on his listeners to come forward at the end of his sermon, Abigail felt herself responding physically. "I cried," she said. "There was a sense that what he was saying was true. I had to decide whether God was primary in my life or just a luxury I could turn to when the going got rough."

Unaware of what anyone around her was doing, she stepped out into the aisle and walked down several flights of stairs toward the platform where the evangelist was beckoning. As she moved forward, she became conscious of streams of other people moving in the same direction. At some point as she drew closer to Graham, Abigail had a definite sense that she should become a pastoral minister.

"I believe God was speaking to me directly, calling me to the ministry," she said. "It didn't occur to me that the idea of going into the ministry was odd, even though I had always been oriented more toward marriage than toward a career. My father was an ordained minister, but he had always been in education, not in a pastorate. And I had never met a woman minister or heard of one, so there was no role model in my background."

Abigail, who was in her late teens at the time, never thought about entering any other career than the ministry after that experience. But when she told people about her decision to become a pastor, she began to run into the same kind of naysaying that Druecillar Fordham and other women have faced. Abigail returned to her home in North Dakota soon after the experience at the Graham rally, and by chance she arrived on the day that a high official of the Presbyterian Church had dropped by her family's home for dinner.

Bubbling with enthusiasm, she told him, "I've decided to become the pastor of a church."

With a sour look on his face, he shook his head: "Forget that idea.

If you want to go to seminary, you can write theology or do Christian education or something. But forget about the pastorate because it isn't realistic for a woman."

Confronted with this verbal wet blanket, Abigail fell silent and evaluated her situation. She knew she still wanted to be a pastoral minister, no matter what this man said, and the Presbyterian Church had opened ordination to women in 1956. But she realized that to achieve her goal, she would have to be firm in her resolve and prepare to overcome some difficult obstacles.

Abigail entered Princeton Seminary in 1958, and one of the first things she heard from the male students was, "Aw, you're just here to catch a husband." In seeming fulfillment of this prediction, she did marry her husband, Bob, during her first year in seminary, and they left for Brazil to serve as missionaries for several years.

"When we were first married, he'd make these glib statements about marrying me to save the church from another woman minister," she said. "That was kind of an 'in' thing with his friends—an inside joke. He had biblical objections to women in the ministry when we were first married, but he never told me point blank he didn't want me to be a minister. He'd mention Bible verses, such as those saying women should be silent in church and so forth, but we didn't get into a real examination of biblical material."

As Abigail worked side by side with Bob in Brazil doing evangelism and pastoral work, his attitude changed. "I think the practicalities of Brazil helped alter his thinking," she said. "He encouraged me to study with Karl Barth at the University of Basel in Switzerland while he was working on his doctorate. And when we returned to the States he got into the radical left bag as a supporter of such causes as the grape and lettuce boycotts and the women's rights movement." Abigail went on to get her bachelor of divinity degree from Princeton Seminary and was ordained as a Presbyterian minister. She is now a tenured associate pastor at the Broadway Presbyterian Church in New York City.

Druecillar Fordham also had to overcome some skepticism in her family when she decided to become a preacher. As a young woman from South Carolina, she did some traveling with a gospel singing group, and her father heartily approved of that activity. But when she moved to New York City and told him she was going to start her own church, he said, "It's all right for a woman to sing and pray—but not preach! Preaching is too hard for a woman."

"Well, Dad, everybody has a right to his own thinking," she replied.

Thinking back on those early encounters with her family, Druecillar, who pastors the hundred-member Christ Temple Church, said, "I just kept on doing what I was doing. By the time my father made his second trip to New York, he was my best audience. He came around. The whole family did. My sister at first acted like 'she ain't got good sense,' but she's come around. My nieces are members here now, even though they don't live here."

Getting a family member to "come around," as Druecillar puts it, can sometimes involve serious arguments and even tears. Diane Pierce, a bespectacled, determined young Congregational minister from Connecticut, said she had to steel herself on the night of her ordination because her mother broke down into tears and cried, "It's all my fault."

"What do you mean?" Diane asked.

According to Diane, the story her mother told went like this: When her mother was in her early forties, she had already been married for seventeen years, and though she desperately wanted children, the doctors had told her she couldn't. A friend of hers who was a Catholic said, "Why don't you pray?" As a last resort, Diane's mother asked the Lord to give her a daughter: "If you're there, Lord, give me a daughter, and I'll give her back to you."

"She never told me that story until the night of my ordination," Diane said. "She seemed heartbroken that she had said that prayer because she had never wanted me to enter the ministry. My faith had always been a private thing to me, but I felt a definite call to the ministry when I was in junior high school and decided to write that commitment down in the eighth-grade yearbook. When I told my mother what I was going to do, she tried to talk me out of it—said I was going to be a freak and the boys weren't going to want to date me. I went ahead and had that printed under my picture, and, as it turned out, she was right. You'd be surprised how saying you want to be a minister can cut into your social life! My mother is more sympathetic now, but she thought it was a real calamity at the time of my ordination."

Unlike Diane, Connie Parvey, a lanky, honey-blond Lutheran pastor who has a penchant for wearing slacks and leather vests with her clerical collar, didn't encounter family resistance to her decision to become a minister. But she did wander for years through several careers, unable to find her occupational niche because her denomination, the Lutheran Church in America, wouldn't open up ordination to women until 1970.

She had always been "service-oriented" and found as a high school and college student in the Midwest that she was constantly asking the question "why" when other students were trying to answer the question "how." One of her college deans at the University of Minnesota suggested that she should pursue religious studies on a Danforth Fellowship at Vanderbilt University in Nashville, Tennessee, and she decided to follow his advice.

Connie spent the next few years in a variety of campus ministry jobs from North Carolina to Wisconsin, and picked up divinity school credits at Union Theological Seminary in New York City and at the Harvard Divinity School. Finally, she qualified for her bachelor of divinity degree at Harvard in 1962, but there was no place for her to go. Her male classmates headed into the ordained ministry, but as a Lutheran, she couldn't be ordained. Ironically, she was told she was "overqualified" for one campus ministry job, but she finally found another position in the Midwest working with Lutheran students at the University of Wisconsin. She soon realized, though, that she couldn't move up to a position of greater responsibility without getting ordained.

"I decided at that point that I was no longer going to work for the church," she said. "I was getting stomach ulcers, and I thought, 'The hell with this! I've been in this work now for twelve years, and if I'm not given the chance to move up to the next level, then I've done everything I can.'"

Connie quit her campus ministry job and started doing some television work with a local station. Eventually, she returned to the Harvard Divinity School to do some teaching and writing. When the Lutheran Church in America announced that ordination would be opened to women in 1970, she jumped at the chance. One church leader she consulted said, "Oh, Connie, you don't want to get ordained. You don't want to get yourself in that box."

"I don't necessarily think of the ministry as a box," replied Connie, who was approaching forty and was in no mood to play the shrinking violet after waiting years for this opportunity. "That's the problem— too many ministers *do* think of the ministry as a box. To me, the ministry is a platform that makes it possible to do a great many things —create a great deal of change."

But the waiting wasn't over for her. In the Lutheran Church it's necessary for prospective ministers to submit their names to the church authorities and then wait for a church to "call" them to a specific job before they can be ordained. "You can have a personal call from here to eternity, but that's not enough in the Lutheran Church," she explained. "I had a personal call my whole life, in a sense, because I've always been a service-oriented, ministry-oriented person. But in the Lutheran Church, a community must recognize that they want you in a priestly, pastoral role, or you won't get ordained."

Connie sat around for two years until she learned that her home church, the University Lutheran Church in Cambridge, Massachusetts, was looking for an associate pastor. She submitted her own name and asked to be considered for the position and was finally accepted. "I think the only reason I did receive a call here is that I had spent six years in this church, and a lot of people knew me and my work. They were willing to risk experimenting with me."

But even if the way is theoretically open for ordination from the official, denominational point of view, the biggest roadblocks of all to women may be erected by lay people. Take the situation faced by Abigail Evans.

After her stint with her husband as a missionary in Brazil, Abigail was ordained as a Presbyterian minister in eastern Kentucky. She worked there as a circuit-riding preacher for two years while her husband taught in a college. Then they moved to the New York City area with their four sons, and Abigail started looking for a permanent pastoral position. After trying several blind alleys, she finally found that Manhattan's Broadway Presbyterian Church, which serves the Columbia University community, was interested in her for a part-time position. But during interviews with several committees at the church, she had to respond to a barrage of suspicious questions.

"Do you think you can work at this and still take care of your four boys?" one man asked.

"Yes, I know I can do it," she responded.

"How about being a woman—wouldn't that be a hindrance?"

"No, I think it would be an asset," she said.

"How's that?"

"First of all, the majority of church members are women. Secondly, I think there's an innate feminine ability to care and be concerned and open to people—an ability that isn't necessarily true of a man."

Her arguments finally won over the church committees, and she was hired. Her work was so well received that she eventually was made a full-time associate pastor, which is a tenured position at the church.

Reverend Evans is not the only female minister who has had to have a ready answer for skeptical members of lay committees. Joanne Whitcomb, a tall young woman with an ironic sense of humor, was ordained by the United Methodist Church, which has ordained women as pastors with full clergy rights since 1956. But she encountered resistance when she graduated from seminary and started looking for a job at a regional Methodist meeting in Ohio.

One layman, who was a member of a committee that was looking for a pastor, asked, "Do you think you'd have trouble at a church social deciding whether you should be in the kitchen with the women or out in the hall talking with the men?"

"I certainly hope every person would help in whatever way possible in a situation like that," she replied with a twinkle in her eye. "I think there might be some men in the kitchen and some women talking in the hall. What do you think?"

He chuckled at her answer, and she was eventually hired by his church in Easthampton, Massachusetts. "I consider myself a feminist —it's an important and serious thing to me," she reflected later. "But I don't think I'm very threatening to people. At least, I don't attempt to be."

Sometimes a good sense of humor and a quick, clever answer to a tough parishioner's question isn't enough to land a job. Rabbi Sally Priesand, who was ordained as the first female rabbi in the United States in June 1972, even had trouble getting some Reform synagogues to interview her. "They made it clear to my school officials that they didn't want to talk to me because I was a woman," she said.

Other synagogue committees would give her an interview and then at the end say, "Well, our congregation just isn't ready to have a woman rabbi." One rabbi, who was interviewing candidates to be his assistant, was having trouble making up his mind and started thinking out loud as the interview proceeded: "Well, I don't think I'd want a woman to do things I'd want my assistant to do, like go to a cemetery on a cold day or visit someone at night. You know, those kinds of things."

Sally found his attitude to be "ridiculous," but she respected him for being straightforward. "I wrote to him after the interview and said I was sorry he felt that way, but at least he had been honest."

After several false starts, she did manage to land some temporary jobs while she was studying at the Hebrew Union College-Jewish Institute of Religion in Cincinnati, Ohio. One opening appeared at a synagogue in Illinois, where the regular rabbi had moved on and an interim rabbi was needed for a few months. She later learned that before she went there for an interview, the secretary of the synagogue had polled the members of the congregation by saying, "I'm going to ask you a question, and I want to know what *you* think about it—*not* what you think everybody else will think. Now here's the question: what would you think about having a woman as a temporary rabbi for this congregation?"

Most replied, "It's fine with me, but I don't think anybody else will want it."

Laughing as she recounted the story, Sally said, "They were waiting for everybody else to say no, and they ended up with me. They were very warm and hospitable after I got there. After my first service, a little girl came up to me and said, 'You know, you're an okay rabbi.' That meant a lot to me after all those years of study."

Sally eventually found a permanent position as an assistant rabbi at the Stephen Wise Free Synagogue in Manhattan, where she has encountered almost no resistance because she's a woman. "I only needed one congregation to accept me, and I always knew I'd find that one congregation. When I came here to be interviewed for the job, I was so impressed with the rabbi and the principles on which the synagogue is based that I really couldn't say no."

Most women ministers who are out looking for their first pastorates have to operate on their own, without help from any man. But a few have husbands who are also ordained in their denominations, and that can sometimes make job-hunting a little easier—but not always. Jim and Susan Gertmenian, who are ordained Presbyterian ministers, seemed to have a great deal going for them when they started being interviewed for pastoral positions in New York and New England. They talked to several church committees and got a number of favorable responses. One New England church in particular interested them, but they made it clear to the committee that they wanted to share equally in all of the pastoral duties, including the preaching. The church, after hearing them both preach, offered a job, and they immediately phoned the other churches at which they had been interviewed to break off further negotiations. They got through to all the other churches except a small parish in Afton, New York, because the chairman of the Afton committee was away from home when they called.

But then a shock came from the church that had accepted them: "The committee there got in touch and said they wanted me to do most of the preaching," Jim said. "They felt their congregation wouldn't want a woman to do much preaching. The excuse they gave was that Susan's trial sermon had been a little more 'radical' than mine."

Angered about the incident, Susan said, "I felt like ripping them to shreds! I was furious. I said you can just take your job and throw it out the window!"

"We were quite angry, all right," Jim agreed.

"We let them know all through the interview that we would share the preaching and everything else equally," Susan said. "This was understood. Then this sneaky little move at the end—I'm glad they did that because I wouldn't have wanted us to go there after seeing how they operated."

But after they rejected this church, they realized they were left without any place to go because they had turned down all the others—except the congregation in Afton, New York. They immediately got on the phone and found that the members there were not only prepared for a husband-wife team, but were actually enthusiastic about it.

"It was really a stroke of Providence," Susan said.

"Yes, this was the one place we hadn't said no to because we couldn't get in touch with the guy," Jim said. "We both really believe the Spirit of God moved to bring us to this place. We had really fought it because we had romantic ideas about New England and that scene. But we were directed back here. It's easy to say in retrospect that God was working, but I believe he was."

Jim and Susan were under considerable pressure because both of them were recent seminary graduates without a church base which they could fall back on if their negotiations failed. But what if Jim had already been pastor of a church and wanted Susan elevated to an equal position as his co-pastor? At first glance, an ordained wife with a husband who is already pastor of a church would seem to have a great advantage in her efforts to move into a co-pastor's position. But Harry and Judy Hoehler, who are both ordained Unitarian ministers, found that arrangement didn't automatically solve all their problems. Harry, solidly built and cerebral, was the pastor of the historic First Parish of Weston, Massachusetts, and Judy, a top graduate of the first Harvard Divinity School class to admit women, was the church's Director of Religious Education. Since their children had reached adolescence, they decided that the time had come for the willowy, black-haired Judy to take over more duties at the church and be designated as a co-pastor alongside her husband.

"We took a sabbatical in England and began to rethink our roles in the church," Harry said. "There had been some talk about an associate or assistant minister, but Judy was operating as a second minister already. She was doing considerable counseling and preaching. And she was carrying on some of the committee work and representing the church in the community. So we worked up a proposal to have ourselves designated as co-pastors."

When they presented the idea to the congregation, many people were in favor of it, but there was also a certain amount of opposition. "I think the opponents had the most difficulty with the philosophical issue of making the woman the equal of the man," Judy said.

The opposition often surfaced in disguised, subtle ways. One question which kept cropping up was, "What happens if we have this co-equal ministry and either Harry or Judy dies?"

The real, unstated concern in the question, though, was this: "Suppose Harry dies and the church is left with just Judy, a woman minister?"

Harry explained that those voicing this objection "were willing to accept the idea of a co-ministry, but they weren't sure about a woman alone. We told them this was a particular kind of ministry we had proposed, and it would exist only as long as the two of us were co-ministers. A co-pastor arrangement wouldn't mean the continuation of either one of us alone."

One of the most interesting reasons offered by the opposition was the argument that co-ministers, like co-chairmanships, are not good managerial models. "There are a lot of faculty members and businessmen in our parish, and this was a basis for uneasiness among them," Judy said.

Harry met this objection with the explanation that "the managerial model we've proposed has been working for the last three years. Some people still look at the minister as the head of the church. But this is a church that runs mainly on its lay committees. On the managerial side, I look on a minister as an enabler who sees that committees are functioning and giving information to each other. The pastor provides the direction the church takes. In our situation, the minister is not the head, or the chief executive of the board, however."

Judy and Harry fielded these and other arguments in a rational, calm way, without trying any church power politics. "No confrontation tactics were used," Harry said. "In the first place, they wouldn't have succeeded. In the second place, we just didn't want to approach the problem that way. We discussed our proposal at a three-hour meeting and said we felt a co-ministry would add strength to the parish. We stressed that both Judy and I would be able to look at the parish and ourselves in a different way."

In the face of their persistent but low-key approach, the opposition finally disappeared and the church's annual meeting voted to call Judy as a co-minister. The actual language of the call was that they were called as "ministers of the First Parish," rather than as "co-ministers," so that each could sign documents for weddings and other official events just as "minister."

Even when a congregation like Judy Hoehler's has been won over, the fight for female acceptance may not be finished. Women pastors often must also do battle with an even more skeptical group—male ministers in the surrounding community. Druecillar Fordham, for example, found that neighboring ministers in Harlem refused to accept her as a colleague. One brusque male pastor said, "I don't believe God called you to preach."

"I don't think he called you either," she replied. "God doesn't call people, he anoints them." As the man, looking disconcerted, stopped for a moment to absorb her rejoinder, she continued: "An anointing to preach is something you feel. It's an urge that makes you want to go out to tell the good news to other people, to help the less fortunate, the widows and the children."

"Who ordained you?" the male preacher asked.

"I didn't ask who ordained you—why do you want to know who ordained me?"

Realizing he was not going to convince her, the man finally said, "God never called any woman to preach. I wouldn't let you preach in my pulpit, I know that much."

"Well, I don't *need* a pulpit to preach," Druecillar said emphatically. "I could preach in the streets if I have to. Jesus never had a pulpit. He preached in the boat, on the mountain, wherever he got a crowd—that's where he spoke. I don't have to have a pulpit either."

Nor is Druecillar Fordham the only female minister whose parish ministry has been opposed by male pastors. Ruth Thompson, who has served as the president of an association of Massachusetts Baptist churches, almost didn't get ordained because several ministers tried to block her entry into the pastoral ministry. As a young woman, she entered Andover-Newton Theological School but got married and pregnant before she could graduate.

Having worked as an assistant to a minister and as director of Christian education in several churches, she felt qualified when the First Baptist Church of Gardner, Massachusetts, asked her to fill in as interim pastor in the mid-1950s. Ruth found the idea of a pastorate attractive because her husband, who was an ordained minister, had left pastoral work to become a traveling fund-raiser. The prospect of a full-time church position promised to fill up the lonely days while he was on the road, so she decided to accept the offer.

After she had worked in the church for several months, the congregation decided she was so good that they wanted her to become their regular pastor. Although most American Baptist ministers have seminary degrees, some exceptions are made for those with practical pastoral experience. Since Ruth fit into that category, she didn't expect any problems in getting ordained, especially since American Baptists have been ordaining women since the late nineteenth century. But she hadn't counted on the opposition of local male pastors.

"These men were part of an association of clergymen who have to approve applications for ordination," she said. "They told my church, 'We're not about to ordain her right away. You let her have the church for a year, and if the church is still in business, we'll talk about it.' It was so strange—my husband and I still laugh about it."

But the situation she faced wasn't a laughing matter at the time because the opposing male pastors said they wanted to talk to Ruth's lay people without her being present. "It's peculiar to call the lay people together without the candidate being present," she explained. "They would never have done that to a man. But they seemed very upset that I didn't have a bachelor of divinity degree. They never really said they objected because I was a woman, but that was evident to me."

Ruth told some of her key lay leaders, "You should tell them they can come and see you, but say you've called me as your pastor and under no circumstances will you talk to them without me."

The other ministers agreed to Ruth's being present, and at the outset of the interrogation, one of the pastors asked, "Ruth, who's going to do your housework if you take this job?"

"You know, I've been around this association for about six years in my husband's congregations," she replied. "I've been in nearly every parsonage around here, and ours has always been one of the best-looking, best-cared-for homes. I don't think it's going to be any harder to take care of it now than it was before."

Her deacons seemed more convinced than ever that she should become their permanent pastor after this meeting, but she still decided not to push her ordination. "Look, the only thing I can't do without ordination is to marry people, and there's no one waiting to be married now," she told her lay leaders. "Let's not worry too much about it."

The lay people were less patient, though, and they sent a delegation to Boston to talk to church officials there. But Ruth decided to wait at least a year and let the controversy blow over. She was ordained about a year later, and eventually came to be accepted even by those pastors who had opposed her. Ironically, on the night of her ordination, several of the lay people in her church began to express doubts about her ordination, but for an entirely different reason than she would have expected.

"I saw some of the church women standing off to one side just before the ceremony, and they were in tears," she said. "I told my husband to go over and see what was bothering them." After he had talked to them for a few moments, he returned with a slight smile on his face. "They said if you get ordained, some other church will come and take you," he reported.

Ruth told him, "Go back and tell them not to worry a bit. Did they ever hear of a church that was looking for a woman?—ask them that. The only churches that ever actually seek out a woman are ones like this, where we go in as interim pastors. After we've been there a few months, the people say, 'That's not too bad! We could live with that!' "

Ruth Thompson's observation was undoubtedly accurate in the 1950s, and it's still true to a large extent today. Many lay people would never make it a point to consider a woman pastor if a qualified —or even half-qualified—male preacher were available. But times are changing, and the exceptions to her generalization may yet prove the rule.

One of the most striking examples of shifting grass-roots attitudes involves a United Methodist church in Chicago—the Parish of the Holy Covenant. The members of this congregation had been favorably impressed with several female seminary students who had worked with them. Also, "We were very conscious of the feminist movement, particularly as it relates to job opportunities," explained Ethel Vrana, the chairperson of the church's Council on Ministries (executive committee of the governing body, the Administrative Board). "Many of us in the congregation are working women, and we just decided that since our senior pastor was leaving, it would be appropriate for us to ask for a woman pastor."

The pastor-parish committee and several other leaders of the church convinced the rest of the members that a woman pastor was a good idea, and in the summer of 1974 they made a formal request to the district superintendent. The superintendent, however, said he was unable to find any women with the experience that the Holy Covenant Church required. The church members agreed reluctantly to accept a male pastor on a temporary basis, but they were not willing to let the matter drop. They arranged for a couple of meetings with the local Methodist bishop and demanded a written agreement with the bishop to encourage the hiring of women pastors in the area's Methodist churches. They also continued to request a female pastor for their own congregation.

"The bishop agreed that within a year he would try to have ten experienced women pastors in our regional conference," explained Masao Yamasaki, the church's lay leader. "There are more women members in our churches than men, but these women are not being represented. Giving a voice to those who should be given a voice is one of the things we were pushing."

Ethel Vrana said that the most exciting part of the experience for her was to see "there were men in the congregation who were willing to stand up and be counted. We had a congregational meeting so that the bishop could see how strong we were. He found an articulate congregation who had done their homework."

As a result of this show of force, the bishop agreed to a second meeting with the pastor-parish committee, and the two sides worked out an agreement that laid the groundwork for hiring qualified female pastors in the future. "I can't think of any member of the church who was absent the night the bishop visited with us," Ethel Vrana said. "When it came down to the wire, everybody agreed. We put up a united front. Outside the church, you have government and private organizations pushing for the equality of women, just as they did for minority groups. But in the church, you really have nobody. You have to rely on the good will of people—both men and women—to conduct themselves as Christians who believe in the principle of equality."

The willingness of Ethel Vrana and her fellow church members to take a tough stand for women's rights in the church finally paid off just a year after the agreement with the bishop. A female pastor was assigned at that time to the parish.

Grass-roots pressure from congregations like Chicago's Parish of the Holy Covenant is becoming a key factor in opening up opportunities for women in the pastoral ministry. And women do seem to have a better chance to land a pastoral job now than they did a few years ago. But as a practical matter, most of them have to settle for positions as pastors of small, rural churches, or as associate or assistant pastors of large congregations. Rarely do they have an opportunity to display their talents as the head pastors of large urban or suburban churches. If lay people are to accept women as pastors on equal terms with men, they have to be educated. A growing feminist movement in the church is using both subtle and not-so-subtle weapons to mold positive attitudes among the masses of church members.

CHAPTER THREE

"Our Mother Who Art in Heaven . . ."

As Arabella Meadows-Rogers pulled up her long black caftan and dropped to her knees, the moderator turned to the congregation and said, "All ordained ministers and elders who wish to participate in the laying on of hands in this ordination are invited to come forward."

Dozens of ministers—most of them women—moved to the front of the sanctuary on the campus of New York's Union Theological Seminary, and leaned forward to touch the small smiling young woman with the pixie hairdo who bowed before them. One of the women carried a squirming infant on her hip. Carter Heyward, the irregularly ordained Episcopal priest, crowded in with the others. Arabella's ordination to the Presbyterian ministry was a thoroughly female affair and symbolized a growing feminist trend in Christian churches.

Of the thirteen official participants in the ceremony, eight were female. Some of the songs exuded the overriding theme of women's liberation:

> Sometimes I wish my eyes hadn't been opened
> But now that they have I'm determined to see
> That somehow my sisters and I will be one day
> The free people we were created to be.
>
> (CAROLE ETZLER, 1974)

The woman who delivered the sermon, Union Professor Beverly Wildung Harrison, even apologized at one point for making a positive reference to the Apostle Paul, whose remarks about women being silent in the church have made many feminists regard him as their nemesis. Arabella's tall, blond husband, Rob, who is the pastor of a United Methodist church, entered into the spirit of the event by offering "words of support" at one point in the service.

"Arabella, the support which I offer you today is that of a friend, and brother, and husband," he declared in part. "I hope to give you and me and us the room to grow and—adamantly untrue to the traditional husbandly duty—I shall not strive to put any manner of roof over or on top of either of our heads. I love you and will continue to love you as the free woman God created you to be."

The service was much more than just an ordination ceremony. It was a celebration of female consciousness in the church—a consciousness which is inspiring young ministers like Arabella to attempt to reform church attitudes, but which is also evoking reactions that range from boredom, to annoyance, to unmitigated fury among traditionalists.

Committed feminists in the clergy often begin their attack on male chauvinism at the most basic level—the man's eye for a sexy female figure. Polly Laughland, a fifty-year-old Unitarian minister who is as outspoken about women's rights as many colleagues half her age, uses the stony-faced-stare ploy to discourage lecherous remarks made in her presence. She was near two male ministers who were sitting together at a church conference. Both the men were concentrating hard on a shapely female church official who was sitting on the speakers' platform in front of them.

"Hey, I'm having a little trouble concentrating on the proceedings up there," one of the men said as he gave an evil wink to his companion.

"Yeah," the other minister replied, grinning. "Well, if she was my secretary and crossed her legs like that, I couldn't keep my mind on my work either."

They looked in Polly's direction, apparently to see if she thought their remarks were humorous, but she set her lips in a firm, stern line and looked at them as if to say, "Come on, boys, grow up!"

Such sexual comments echo more often than the average layperson realizes through the hallowed halls of ministers' meetings, and in recent years an increasing number of women preachers have been introduced—or subjected—to this kind of humor. Polly Laughland has heard every variety of sexist joke. With a condescending sigh, she says she has found the best response is "just to keep a straight face." As she sees it, a joke without laughter is not a joke at all.

But more often than not, the proper feminist education of "unliberated" churchmen requires explicit persuasion and exhortation. As part of this *ad hoc* learning program, some women pastors constantly correct men who use sexist language, and they stage outright confrontations when necessary to make a feminist point.

A classic example of a confrontation over the sexist language issue involved Jean Gilbert, a New York City hospital chaplain who has been ordained as an elder by the United Methodist Church. She was assigned to supervise some men who were trying to sharpen their skills in pastoral care, and at the beginning of the sessions, one man said to her, "Well, it looks like you're going to be the only girl in the group."

"I'm not a girl," she replied. "I'm a woman."

"Okay, don't get excited," the man replied. "I don't think there's anything wrong with calling a young woman in this context a girl."

"How would you like it for me to call you 'boys'?" she answered heatedly.

"Now you're being immature, getting offended at something like this."

They spent about an hour discussing why it was important for Jean to be called a woman, and it was unlikely that the men who participated in the discussion would ever forget it. Their education in the pitfalls of sexist language had begun.

A similar encounter occurred during an interview between a male journalist and the Reverend Bonnie Jones-Goldstein, who is the chairperson of the Commission on the Status and Role of Women of the United Methodist Church's New York Annual Conference. Bonnie was describing her first parish experience as a pastor in the Catskills and the man commented, "It must have been fairly lonely up there for a young single woman."

"Yes, it was," she replied.

"Did you have any girl friends?"

"Women friends."

"What's that?" the journalist asked.

"Women friends. I don't consider myself a girl. I consider myself a woman. I'm beginning to feel real anger about the language both inside and outside the church."

The man laughed nervously and changed the subject, but his careful choice of words during the rest of the interview showed he had received the message.

The battle against sexist language has also invaded the worship services in a number of churches. Joanne Whitcomb, who pastors a Methodist church in Easthampton, Massachusetts, selected a responsive reading for one service which began, "God created man out of the dust of the earth." But instead of reading the words as they were written, she said, "God created man *and woman* out of the dust of the earth."

After the service, one couple pulled her aside and asked, "Don't you believe in Genesis?"

"What are you referring to?" Joanne, a tall, twenty-nine-year-old with a disarming sense of humor, replied innocently.

"In the Bible it says God created man out of the dust of the earth and Eve out of the rib of Adam. Don't you believe that?"

"No," Joanne said simply, and the elderly man and woman smiled slightly and walked out.

Joanne explained later that "those two weren't upset, and I knew they wouldn't be. They were just partially serious in their question. I believe those verses in Genesis were a poetic statement, written millions of years after those things actually happened. But when you're shaking hands at the door of the church, it's not the best time to go into detail about the precise way you interpret verses like that."

Joanne, who likes to wear slacks and a turtleneck when she's not in the pulpit, has also carried her crusade against male-oriented language into the administrative meetings at her church. On one occasion, a man asked, "Lois is chairman of the council on ministries, isn't she?"

"How can Lois be chairman?" Joanne asked as she thoughtfully fingered an ornate silver cross around her neck.

The man stopped short, looked at her for a moment as though she were crazy, and then an expression of understanding crossed his face.

"I mean chair*person*," he replied self-consciously.

For Joanne, this kind of educational process is not simply nitpicking. "Language in general is very important to me," she explained. "It conditions the way your mind works. I think people don't realize what an effect it has. Most important things are expressed in male terms. If a student applies to such-and-such college, *he* is expected to do this or that. The female child somehow gets obliterated by never getting mentioned. I think that's a very important and harmful tendency. Language is where I draw the line between those who take the feminist issue seriously and those who don't."

Joanne has been so persistent in her church that some men even correct each other if the word "chairman" comes up instead of "chairperson." "They're very conscious of this problem when I'm sitting in meetings with them," she said. "When they talk about the minister in the abstract, they always say 'he or she' instead of just saying 'he.' You'd have to be a complete thickhead to use male pronouns when a female minister is sitting next to you.

"We also use the word 'layperson' too, instead of 'layman.' 'Layman' is a heavily masculine word and reflects the way the church has been organized."

Church music has also been a target of the feminist onslaught. "It's hard to use the hymn book without sexist language," commented Unitarian minister Polly Laughland. "I don't make a big deal out of it, but sometimes I'll say, 'Please sing the second and fourth verses with feminine pronouns.' One man behind me in the choir didn't dig that very much. I heard him say, 'We might as well call them all "it." '"

Connie Parvey, associate pastor of a Lutheran congregation in Cambridge, Massachusetts, came close to provoking a similar reaction when she chose the hymn "Turn Back, O Man, Forswear Thy Foolish Ways" for one Sunday service.

When she stood up to preach, she noticed she was getting some hostile stares from the congregation, so she remarked, "I can see I got some dirty looks, but I don't have any trouble with that hymn at all. That's one of the best hymns in the hymnal."

The congregation broke up in laughter, and the tension lifted. One male visitor told her afterward, "I like the tender way you handle my male-chauvinist-pig attitudes."

Although the Protestant denominations have a longer history of women in the pulpit than any other religious group, female rabbis are also beginning to make some contributions to the fight for new liturgies in the Jewish services. Sandy Sasso, who is the rabbi of the Manhattan Reconstructionist Havurah, or fellowship, was instrumental in changing the male-oriented language of a traditional Jewish prayer for her graduation ceremony at the Reconstructionist Rabbinical College in Philadelphia. The original version of the prayer begins like this: "Our God, God of our fathers, God of Abraham, God of Isaac, God of Jacob . . ." Sandy convinced the other students and the faculty that the prayer should be changed to read, "Our God, God of our people, God of Abraham and Sarah, God of Isaac and Rebeccah, God of Jacob, Rachel and Leah . . ."

The Reform tradition of Judaism is also being challenged by Rabbi Sally Priesand. "In the prayer book when I come to the word 'mankind,' I say 'humanity,'" she said. "When I come to 'men,' I say 'people.' Instead of 'God of our fathers,' I insert 'God of our ancestors.' Generally, though, I don't insist on the congregation's making the same changes that I do. I don't think it's fair to confuse them since our prayer books haven't been changed to eliminate the male imagery. But there have been occasions where the members of the congregation have changed the words on their own. As I'm standing in the pulpit, I've heard people change the words when we're all reading together."

Sally is also working on changing the Reform prayer books used by her New York City congregation and has been in touch with the liturgy committee of the Central Conference of American Rabbis, which consists of Reformed rabbis. "The whole concept of God as a male image is especially difficult," she says. "I'm not convinced yet we need to change God. I don't know how we're going to do it because I can't see referring to God as 'she' or 'it.' The only answer may be to always say 'God,' never to use pronouns."

The tug of tradition overcomes many women ministers at this point because of the deep-rooted, paternal associations most Christians and Jews have with the deity. "I've been more conscious of the problem of God as a father in recent years," says Joanne Whitcomb. "But it touches something positive in me to start a prayer off with 'father.' A minister in my college always did that, and I appreciated it. I still respond emotionally to it, but intellectually, I don't like it. God is Spirit and Truth, and to say God is masculine is to say masculinity is the most important and powerful factor."

Despite the emotional inclination to regard God as a father, there are a number of biblical passages that suggest the deity also has feminine characteristics. The prophet Isaiah, for example, quotes the Lord as saying, "As one whom his mother conforts, so I will comfort you; you shall be comforted in Jerusalem" (Isaiah 66:13). And David writes in Psalm 131, "O Lord, my heart is not lifted up . . . But I have calmed and quieted my soul, like a child quieted at its mother's breast; like a child that is quieted is my soul. O Israel, hope in the Lord from this time forth and for evermore." Christian feminists who believe Jesus is God find further support for this female side of the deity in Christ's cry, "O Jerusalem, Jerusalem, killing the prophets and stoning those who are sent to you! How often would I have gathered your children together as a hen gathers her brood under her wings, and you would not!" (Matthew 23:37; Luke 13:34). Although few ministers would go so far as to affirm a "father-mother God" concept as the Christian Scientists have, we may be witnessing the first steps in this direction in the more traditional Christian denominations.

As the women preachers continue to press their attack, changes are occurring not only in the liturgical language, but also in the very substance of religious rituals. Reform Rabbi Sally Priesand, for example, helped change the way her congregation observed the "festival of the rejoicing of the law." Traditionally, this has been a ceremony where the Torah is passed symbolically from generation to generation by the male members of one of the synagogue's families. The Torah, in other words, passes from grandfather, to father, to son. But Sally succeeded in transforming one of her services so that the Torah was passed from a grandmother to a mother to a daughter.

"The women were from a family that had been brought up in the synagogue," Sally said. "There was no resistance from the other members. Everybody was pleased."

Many women preachers also encourage couples whom they are marrying to remove the word "obey" and all other references to submission from the nuptial ceremony. In fact, Lutheran Connie Parvey said that she would refuse to conduct a wedding if the couple insisted on using the word "obey." "I think it's wrong," she declared. "And if a woman wanted that submission passage, I'd really work with the couple. I wouldn't feel good about starting a marriage out like that. It would be degrading for the woman as a human being. And it could be very bad for the husband too by giving him a false sense of authority."

Changing the form and substance of the worship service is only one tactic in the master strategy of feminist preachers. Many of these pastors have had positive personal experiences in consciousness-raising groups and they're eager for their parishioners to have similar experiences. Carter Heyward, the Episcopal priest, and Jean Gilbert, the Methodist hospital chaplain, both participated in the same consciousness-raising group at Union Seminary. They regard these sessions as decisive in their own discovery of personal identity.

"In that consciousness-raising group, we laid out personal concerns, and since we were all at Union and most of us were 'churchy' kinds of people, we had a common bond," Carter explained. "We began to realize what similar experiences we had as women. It was a mind-opener and -expander for everybody. We began to realize our individual hassles were corporate. None of us was alone. That gives you a lot of strength."

With an approach that almost smacks of spiritual insurgency, Susan Gertmenian, a soft-eyed, casual Californian, has started laying the groundwork for such women's consciousness-raising groups in the blue-collar communities of Nineveh and Afton, New York, where she and her husband are co-pastors of two small Presbyterian churches. She has introduced some of the women in her community to feminist concepts by bringing up the issue at meetings of the Presbyterial, a local church women's organization.

"This group is organized to help with mission work—they sew for people in India and other parts of the world, and raise funds," the long-haired, dungaree-clad brunette said. "There are about twenty woman who attend our local meetings and they asked me to do a program for them."

This was just the opening she had needed. She showed a slide and tape show entitled "Eve and Us," which supported the argument that women are kept out of the decision-making processes of the church.

"These women are pretty self-satisfied," notes Susan, who knits her brows when pondering such problems. "They think they aren't oppressed. Their tendency is to want to give, give, give to these various causes. But I think the feminist perspective is to get to know yourself and what your own personal needs are. I want them to share more with the other people at these meetings. These women have lived together since they were children. They grew up in the same church together, yet they hide a lot of their hurt and anger and joy from each other. As their pastor, I'd like to see them stop feeling that they've always got to go outside of themselves—that's a real avoidance of what's inside."

Susan's strong feminist orientation is rooted both in her interpretation of the Scriptures and in her affirmation of the secular women's liberation movement. "If I dig deep into almost any passage in the New Testament, I find that God is directing me to be my true self," she explained. "Sin enters in when you deny that self and get into obsessive-compulsive behavior to avoid breaking out of patterns and societal pressures. But apart from the Scriptures, I identify, in a sense, with Gloria Steinem. I think her crusade is to get women to appreciate themselves as who they are. Having freedom to choose and not having to respond to anyone else's pressure—that's what I identify with."

Susan's efforts to enlighten the women in her congregation have been low-key, for the most part. Her husband and co-pastor, Jim, a stocky young man with long, black hair, says, "She doesn't come on strong as the feminist flag-bearer. She makes the right points and says the right things at the right time. But her willingness to live in the situation and let it grow is what has made our experience in this community as good as it has been."

His wife agrees that she has been consciously careful not to alienate her parishioners by doing anything that would hint of bra-burning. "I wanted to get along with the people and avoid erecting any barriers so that when the time came they would trust me. Now, some of them are ready to hear me say, 'Mr. So-and-So, why do you let your wife do the dishes every night?' "

Some of the women have started to open up more to her, although "not to each other so much. They've been kept from doing things because they always felt they had to be good mothers or wives or churchwomen. It's been sacrilegious for them to step outside those roles. They feel it's not right for them to have confidence in themselves. That's very frustrating to me, and I'd like for them to motivate themselves by taking a closer look at Jesus' attitude toward women in the Scriptures."

In one conversation, Susan commented to a small group of women that "some of the things Jesus did and said reflect what's going on today in the women's movement."

"I don't see that," one middle-aged matron said curtly.

"I mean the way he deals with some situations, as in the Martha and Mary passage," Susan said. She went on to explain that in Luke 10:38–42, Jesus put a higher value on Mary's interest in discussing matters of faith than he did on Martha's primary concern about housework.

The pressure Susan has been applying has finally, after a year on the job, resulted in a few signs of soul-searching among some of her parishioners. "There are a couple of cases of younger couples where the wife is really dissatisfied because she's talented in more things than just nursing her baby," Susan said. "The women have ambitions and want to fulfill them. The husbands, though, feel it's plain wrong for these women to feel that way. These problems are just in the awakening stages, and I find I'm becoming threatening to the men. That's a limitation I have, and I hope Jim's perspective will help with this."

Susan plans to push even harder to achieve her objectives in the church by joining forces with other members of a Presbyterian women's task force and going out two by two to churches in the surrounding area. They plan to talk to women's organizations and give testimonials as to the value of consciousness-raising groups, in order to "stir up" the lay women so that they become more aware of their emotional needs. But Susan has decided there is a built-in difficulty in trying to set up encounter groups in rural parishes: "It's hard for people who live in small towns to really open up with some things they've tried to keep secret all their lives. We've found that if something happens to you here, the whole town knows it, and privacy is very important in sharing relationships in consciousness-raising groups. We've thought these groups might work better in small towns if we mix up the groups with people from several different villages. That way, the woman you disclose everything to on Tuesday night won't be the same woman you'll see on the street on Wednesday morning."

Susan's ambition to form effective consciousness-raising groups in her church has been realized by Bonnie Jones-Goldstein, a freckle-faced Methodist minister with an omnipresent cigarette and a warm, open manner. She is assisting at her husband's church in upstate New York and at the same time is serving as chairperson of a regional United Methodist committee on the role of women.

"I started a consciousness-raising group in our church, and one of the first problems we had to deal with was my relationship with their pastor, who was my husband," she said.

At the outset, she told the other eight women, "I want to be a person in this group. I don't want to have to hold back my discussion just because my husband is your pastor. We as a group will have to deal with that—how you see him and me and our marriage."

After several sessions, Bonnie and the other women started feeling comfortable with each other. As they tentatively disclosed things about their personal lives—their general fears and dissatisfactions with their families and their personal identity problems—they saw that their discussions were being kept confidential, so they became even more trusting and open. Gradually, the most serious problems that these women faced started coming out in the discussion sessions. One woman got up enough courage to tell the others about the unfair way she felt her husband had been treating her.

"Did you get angry at him?" Bonnie asked.

"Not really," the woman replied. "No, I really didn't get mad at all. I just felt hurt."

Bonnie and the others then proceeded to show this woman that it was important to bring out all her feelings, including anger. "She wasn't able to get as angry as she felt," Bonnie explained later. "Anger is the hardest thing for a woman to deal with. It takes time."

Although the women in Bonnie's group keep the details of their conversations private, their husbands become quite curious about what is being discussed. "What did you say about me?" is a typical question that the wives are hit with when they return home. A few of the men in the church are so fascinated they are even talking about starting a men's consciousness-raising group.

"Some of the husbands felt threatened and some of the people in the church made jokes about us at first," Bonnie said. "But we did a worship service in the church last month, and it had a powerful effect. Other women have started becoming attracted to the idea of joining a group themselves. Now we have enough interest to form three groups, where at first only a handful of women were involved.

"Developing one's spirituality, or relationship with God, is very strongly a part of being a woman," she continued. "The trouble with being spiritual—meditating each day on the Scriptures or whatever—is that it tends to be put down by men. Women hide their relationship with God because it's looked down on; it's too emotional. Many men would say, 'This is a practical world, and you have to think practically.' So a woman's spirituality usually stays private, even when she's involved in public worship. If women relate in such a closed way to God, that often dictates how they relate to their children and their husbands.

"But in a group like ours, women can share openly their inner spiritual feelings, and learn how real and important these feelings are. Because of the supportive relationships we've developed, we regard ourselves as equal to men, not inferior. Women need to see themselves more as whole persons. When you begin to see yourself that way, you can more easily understand yourself as a Christian."

But for every woman who expresses ideas like those of Bonnie Jones-Goldstein and Susan Gertmenian, there seems to be another female pastor who violently opposes the influence of the women's liberation movement on the church community.

"I'm not a women's liberationist!" thirty-year-old Congregational pastor Diane Pierce declared vehemently. "I don't believe in the ordination of women either."

Then why did she decide to become ordained?

"I believe that once in a great while a woman will have a call to the ministry, and that call ought to be honored," the opinionated brunette preacher said. "I do feel a definite call, but I don't feel *every* woman has a *right* to be a pastor. I'd like to get away from my call sometimes—deny it, say it's all in my mind. It would be a lot easier to be a secretary or telephone operator and get out of the whole thing."

Diane makes the traditional argument that "the ministry is a man's role. I'm very conscious all the time that I'm fulfilling a man's job. From time to time this is a very uncomfortable position for me. I'm more comfortable running around in slacks, doing the shopping, chatting with people, running the ladies' aid society and the rummage sales. Those things feel natural to me."

Though she's single and lives alone, Diane is a meticulous housekeeper who argues that "a woman's place is in the home! My marriage would come first if I were married. I believe woman was created to bear children, that the family is the center of society—the whole conservative bag. Although many of the women I know in the ministry have been rampant about this women's liberation thing, I don't believe in it. I don't believe in it in any sense. I believe the husband should be the head of the house and the head of the church and the head of society. I voted against Ella Grasso for governor [of Connecticut] because I couldn't take the idea of a woman governor. The Lord has been calling me apart, though, saying I've got to be different."

Presbyterian associate pastor Abigail Evans says she avoids "like the plague" many of the feminist preachers' causes, such as changing masculine language in the liturgy. She acknowledges she has a "very strong personality," but says "in theory I'm a strong believer in my husband as the head of the family." This belief led her to deliver a Mother's Day sermon to her New York City congregation with the theme "woman is the crown; man is the head."

"That sermon inflamed a lot of women in the church," said Abigail, who designed and made the high-necked black robe, with a ruffled white collar which she wears in the pulpit. "They didn't like the sermon too much because they thought I had presented women in an inferior way. But my understanding of the male-female relationship is one of complementarity. When the husband and wife complement one another, conflict in their roles can be eliminated. I think in the husband-wife relationship, the husband should be the head, and the crowning touch should be the woman. It's very freeing, yet doesn't create a desire to exist apart from a man."

Traditional, anti-feminist attitudes have found a concrete, organizational expression in the efforts of the Reverend Druecillar Fordham, who formed what amounts to a non-feminist consciousness-raising group at her Southern Baptist church in Harlem. "Our group, called the United Women Ministers' League, meets twice a month, and consists of women ministers and a few lay people. We have around fifty members now, and we study the Bible and discuss social issues. A few of the young women who attend are aspiring to the ministry. I tell them, 'You have to go to seminary, and you don't fight anybody. You realize you're a woman and thank God you're a woman. Forget liberation. Jesus Christ met the Samaritan woman at the well, and he liberated her right there. You don't have to get up and prove anything to anybody. Just preach. I don't believe in that women's lib.'"

Other opponents of the women's movement in the church argue that many of the women pastors are basically interested in wresting power from men and dominating them. In support of this power-play theory, there is some evidence that female students are increasing their control over seminary life. "At Union Seminary, the women were the visible leaders in the community from my perspective," notes Robert Meadows-Rogers, a recent Union graduate who is a member of the New York Methodists' Commission on the Status and Role of Women. "Most of the men there who had any role in campus leadership learned a lot from the women's movement. But the women seemed to me to be the most innovative and challenging personalities. They were aggressive, and by and large their personalities were more forceful than the men's. Women who enter seminary have had to overcome a lot of role restrictions. They have to be strong, articulate, intelligent people."

What bothers some male preachers is that as more strong, militant women graduate from seminaries, there will be greater pressures on denominations and churches to accept them, instead of men, as pastors. A few observers are even predicting that if present trends continue, the ministry may lose its masculine traditions and become a woman's occupation.

This tension between male and female roles in the ministry has yet to be resolved in the major denominations. But many husband-wife pastoral teams, which are springing up around the country, are achieving a balance of the sexes on a practical level. The experiences of these couples, though by no means conclusive, suggest there may be answers to the problems of competition and misunderstanding between men and women in the clergy.

CHAPTER FOUR

The Pastor's Husband

When the Reverend Bill Harter visited Cairo in the fall of 1973 with the Middle East Task Force of the United Presbyterian Church, he knew he was sitting on a powder keg. He hoped to be able to make some contributions to international ecumenical understanding, but then the powder keg exploded on the holiest Jewish holiday of the year—Yom Kippur, the Day of Atonement. War broke out between the Arabs and Israelis, and Bill found himself in the middle of it.

"The air raids sounded before dawn, and we rushed down the outside staircases of our hotel to the bomb shelters below," he said. "We could see the jet and missile tracks intersecting in the sky to the east of us, and we couldn't help but wonder whether we were going to get hit."

A couple of missiles and rockets went astray and landed in Cairo, and that increased his apprehension. "People began to express the fear that more bombs would land in the city, or that the Israelis were going to attack us. I think that was a foolish fear, but when you're in the middle of a war like that, you never know. There's always an irrational aspect to it, an uncertain dimension that could escalate into anything. It's frightening. It definitely crossed my mind that I might not be going back home."

Back in Margaretville, New York, that fear also crossed the mind of his associate pastor—his wife, Linda, who was pregnant with their fourth child. As she went to bed on that fateful Yom Kippur Saturday night, she knew the bombs were beginning to devastate the desert only a few miles from where Bill was staying. And she also realized that Cairo might become a primary Israeli target if the war escalated. As if her worries about Bill and the natural tension created by her pregnancy weren't enough, she had the responsibility for major services at their two churches the next morning for World Communion Sunday.

Despite these pressures, Linda, a tall woman in her middle thirties with short, gray-flecked hair, fell asleep immediately every night that Bill was in Cairo. What was her secret? "Have you ever read Psalm 121?" she asks. "It says that 'the Lord is your keeper' and that God, 'who keeps Israel, will neither slumber nor sleep.' Now if God is not slumbering and sleeping but is watching over Israel, why should I worry? The Lord is your keeper—that's a promise. I knew the Lord was keeping Bill, whether he lived or died. I did have to face the possibility of his dying. It would have been hard, but if he had died, I could have coped with it."

Linda's most difficult challenge came when she entered the Margaretville church the next morning to conduct services. "That was really tough—keeping composed in the pulpit the next day. I had the same problem when I conducted church services two days after Bill's mother died. I had to gulp a little to be able to keep going."

But she drew on the congregation for support as she launched into her sermon. "You know Psalm 23?" she asked them. "That's been a constant comfort to me because it says, 'Even though I walk through the valley of the shadow of death, I fear no evil . . . Thou preparest a table before me in the presence of my enemies . . . my cup overflows . . .' Now you know Bill, and you know how he likes to eat, so you can be sure that even though he's in the midst of his enemies, he's eating."

As they laughed, she could sense the warmth and support they felt for her. "Everybody in town was upset," she said. "They were prayerfully concerned, and that meant a lot to me."

With the help of a legion of volunteer baby sitters and the willingness of other church members to help out, she completely took over both Bill's church chores and her own during the three weeks that the war delayed his return. She supervised two membership canvasses, two Sunday schools and all the worship services.

"I'll say one thing, what she did that month was a fantastic Christian witness, not only to the parish but to the entire community," Bill said. "I heard dozens of people talking about how brave she was. They knew what she had been going through and could see the power of her personal faith and use of Scripture. Also, she showed how seriously she regards her involvement in the church. And her willingness to rely on others and admit her own weaknesses gave the power of Christ an opportunity to operate through the people who were supporting her."

If both ordained spouses are as competent in crises as Linda Harter proved herself to be, marriage would seem to offer decided practical advantages for all pastors, male and female. For a marriage of pastors can provide each partner not only with a domestic companion, but also with a readily available substitute preacher, should the need arise.

The multiple advantages of marriage for a minister have not escaped the wistful eyes of a number of single female pastors, who respond favorably to the idea of a warm, mutually supportive domestic relationship. "I'd prefer not to be living alone," declared Joanne Whitcomb, the lively, gregarious twenty-nine-year-old Methodist minister who has a church in Easthampton, Massachusetts. "Someone asked me before I came here if I expected to be married. I said I couldn't plan that. I didn't know anyone at that point that I wanted to share my life with. I wouldn't mind it—in fact, I'd like it very much, to have someone I knew well, someone I loved, someone I could share things with.

"But I'd be just as happy if I had some community to live out of—another family or group of people. I hate to fix food just for myself and sit in front of the TV. I'd like to be able to eat with people. I'm a terrible housekeeper, too, so it would be easier for me if the domestic maintenance chores were shared."

Diane Pierce, a rosy-cheeked, thirty-year-old Congregational pastor from Connecticut, would like to get married too. If she does, she believes strongly that the husband should be "the head of the home." But she's pessimistic about her prospects: "I doubt that I'll get married. I think that's one thing I'm meant to give up. It's the hardest thing for me, but I have a conviction that the Lord isn't going to let me get married. It's one of those things that simmers on the back burner for a while. I always thought it would be a horrible thing if the Lord made me give up getting married because marriage always has been such an important thing for me."

She senses that God has told her, "I won't share you with anybody." But she explains, "I don't know if that means if I get married, it will be to somebody who will draw me closer to God. But I've had to come to peace with this issue during the past year. I know now that marriage might be part of the baggage that goes overboard."

Being a single woman can sometimes be a decided disadvantage in trying to find a church position. Linda Harter, for example, was working with one congregation which had just lost its pastor. As the church embarked on the search for a new preacher, a member of the ministerial committee told her, "We'll consider anyone but a single woman. We'll take a black, an Oriental, a Mexican . . . We'd take a husband-and-wife team too, but not a single woman."

But after Linda had worked with this congregation for several months and demonstrated what a competent female minister working alone could do, the committee informed her that they had changed their minds: they would consider a single woman after all.

Single pastors who are seriously considering marriage may find themselves facing a special set of problems. When an unmarried minister gets settled in her career, she often realizes that the man she marries must have certain very specific qualifications. Methodist pastor Norma Rust, a vigorous, intense widow in her early forties, says she'd like to get married again, "but at this juncture I have so much at stake there's a need for me to be choosy. I wouldn't be interested in marrying a fellow who has a job that would keep him in one particular spot. If I'm called to move, I'd want to go. I plan to stay in the ministry. My job is a priority now in my life, and my husband would have to look at it that way too. That may be selfish on my part, but that's the way I feel. Later on, I might be willing to back off and say, 'I've accomplished this much, and I'm satisfied.' I might be willing to follow a husband's desires at that point. But I'd be frustrated the rest of my life if I walked away from my job now without knowing whether I could make it or not."

No matter how careful a woman pastor may be in choosing a mate, some tension is inevitable if both the husband and wife have established clear-cut career patterns. Even the Reverends Linda and Bill Harter, who have carved out a generally workable and compatible career arrangement, occasionally encounter rough spots in the professional and personal relationships.

Linda, who was converted during a Billy Graham rally in the 1950s, is a thoughtful woman who constantly strives for perfection both as a minister and wife. But there never seems to be enough time for her to take care of their four kids, be a model wife and execute her ministerial duties in accordance with the high standards she has set for herself. A complicating factor is that she is sometimes tempted to compare her pastoral performance with that of her husband. "Sometimes I listen to Bill in the pulpit, and I think I'm not going to want to preach again because he's doing such a good job," she confessed. "There probably is a sense of competition there, though I compare myself to Bill more than he compares himself to me."

"I don't feel it any competition at all," Bill said.

"Well, I feel it, and I feel like I come out on the short end of it," Linda rejoined. "I feel competition in personalities too. Bill's approach is very outgoing and gregarious and charismatic. I'm more reserved. I'm not the hot ticket that he is. There are situations when parishioners talk to me but I can tell they really want to talk to Bill. I often tell them that Bill is going to say the exact same thing I do. Sometimes they accept this, other times, they want to talk to Bill. My reaction now is, let 'em. Sometimes, though, I say, 'What in the world am I doing this for if nobody's going to listen to me?' "

When Linda depreciates or underestimates her abilities, Bill is quick to step in and lift her up emotionally. For example, even though she demonstrated exceptional academic skills in college and seminary, she occasionally backs away from complex theological arguments by saying, "You'd best direct that question to Bill."

After one long opinion that Bill gave on the theological relationships between Christians and Jews, Linda sighed and said, "Bill is the scholar of the family. I don't get into this."

"That's false modesty," Bill replied. "She's very competent. She wrote a paper on this which was used for Bible studies in seminary."

This kind of supportiveness that Bill Harter displays is an essential part of any co-pastoring arrangement involving a husband and wife. And sometimes it's the ordained wife, rather than the husband, who provides the support. The youthful Jim Gertmenian, who pastors the Afton, New York, Presbyterian Church with his wife, Susan, says, "There's definitely an issue of professional pride and jealousy. It's not a huge thing, but we both recognize it's there. If Susan preaches a great sermon, and gets some great comments, then I wonder, 'Wow, what am I going to come up with next week?'

"I might comment to Susan, 'Boy, you really did a fantastic job—I haven't preached a sermon that well in months and I don't expect to.' Susan's reaction would be to build me up. She'd say, 'Look, Jim, you remember this time or that time when you did such a good job.' We're very much aware of what we're doing—that in a sense we're playing a game. But it's a very important game. We know we have to support each other."

Although twenty-six-year-old Susan also feels some competition in the pulpit, she senses more friction between her position and Jim's as she ventures into the traditional "male" tasks around the couple's two churches. One day a workman did some work at the Afton church, and he came to the parsonage door to ask for his check for the job.

"Is Jim at home?" he asked.

"No," Susan replied. "Can I help you?"

The man decided to wait to see Jim, and Susan said, "That really got my goat." She had been dealing with this contractor throughout the construction process, and had signed a number of the papers for the job. She had even led the church meeting the night before at which all the final details had been settled. Although she didn't say anything to the man but just fumed about his attitude, she resolved she would take an open stand if a similar situation confronted her again.

She didn't have long to wait. A leading layman called a few days later to discuss some of the other physical problems of the church. He indicated he wanted to talk to Jim about fixing the church furnace, but he didn't offer to discuss the matter with her, "apparently because he thought it was a man's job," Susan believes. "Finally I told him, 'I can probably handle this, and if I can't I'll let you know.'"

The man responded to her immediately, and she knew she had

taken a major step in showing she was capable of handling *all* the parish's problems.

Perhaps the most aggravating problem that Susan Gertmenian has faced is that she's sometimes pegged as the minister's wife, not as a pastor. "I go to the women's meetings at our church because it's a good time to catch up on people I can't visit individually. Also, I try to inject a feminist perspective in the meetings.

"At one of these sessions, an older woman I've been really close to and have had a good relationship with came up to me as the others were leaving. I had made a few comments about the future of the congregation and she said, 'It's so nice because for many years we didn't have a minister's wife.'

"I'd rather be known as your pastor," Susan replied pointedly.

But this woman didn't see any distinction and had no sense that she had hurt Susan or said something that was threatening to her professional identity. "She wanted to let me know she appreciated me, yet she couldn't have said anything any more cutting as far as I was concerned. You counsel with people, preach every other Sunday, lead the administrative meetings, and you're still the pastor's wife."

Susan has found that the best way to deal with this tendency to downgrade her role is to fall back on her sense of humor and laugh at the absurdity of such encounters. "I prefer that approach instead of crying, 'Oh my God, it crushes me,' and going home and gnashing my teeth all evening," she says. "I've decided I'll be their pastor *whatever* they want to call me!"

An interesting variation on the theme of pastoral competition between ordained spouses was described by Arabella Meadows-Rogers, a bubbly Presbyterian minister who is staff associate for women's concerns at the Association of Theological Schools. When her husband, Rob, the pastor of a Methodist church, is serving Communion, she has found she doesn't want to accept the sacrament from him.

"I've never accepted Communion from Rob," she says. "First of all, my concept of Communion is that I prefer to take it in the congregation, but not at the altar, which is the way it's usually served in his church. I have strong feelings about that. But also I can't put Rob in such an authoritarian role. I have taken Communion at the altar before; for example, I took it from the Episcopal women priests in Philadelphia at their ordination and also when they had the

Eucharist service at Riverside Church. It was extremely important for me to take it from them, to accept their sense of authority. But it's important for me *not* to accept Rob's authority.

"At the altar, you must accept your spouse as a representative of Jesus Christ, and that's a very hard thing to do. It wouldn't bother me as much if I took the elements from Rob as we conducted a joint service. I think my objections are wrapped up in seeing Rob as an authoritarian husband."

Perhaps the most radical solution—and in some cases the best— to the problem of competition and conflict is for the ordained husband and wife to work and worship in separate congregations. Reconstructionist Rabbi Sandy Sasso found that when she and her rabbi husband Dennis worked together in a congregation as seminary students, she often was relegated to a subordinate position. "I found that people tended to look at us as one, rather than as two. It was two for the price of one. When we were together, people would tend to address questions to Dennis rather than to me. I didn't butt in because why would I want to contradict my husband, if what he was saying was correct? I began to see myself in a subordinate role. I didn't want to be aggressive in those situations because I wasn't naturally aggressive anyway."

She recalled one instance when a group of people were on the platform at the front of the synagogue, and they wanted to know whether they should lift the Torah up or put it down at a certain point. Both Sandy and Dennis were sitting together on the platform, but the lay people turned to Dennis to ask their question. Sandy sensed this sort of thing was happening more and more often, but she wondered if she was becoming paranoid. "Perhaps nobody else but me notices any problem here," she thought.

Then the rabbinical couple ran into a woman from their synagogue in a grocery store. She had a question about Jewish history, and she addressed the question to Dennis, who immediately gave her an answer. The woman called Sandy later and said, "You know, I always thought I was very liberated. I always got very angry at other people when they didn't view me as an independent, competent person. But I realized after I asked that question this afternoon that I didn't address it to you as well as Dennis, and I'm sorry."

This woman's confession convinced Sandy that she wasn't paranoid, and she decided she had to do something to correct the situation when she and Dennis graduated from seminary in June of 1974 and started looking for permanent jobs. "I was afraid I'd always be in the background," she explained. "More than that, I wouldn't be able to develop my own thoughts and my own image. I was tending to depend on him too much. I wouldn't pay any attention to the questions that were being asked, and that was bad for me. I decided if I could operate independently at first, then I would be viewed as an individual and would have a chance to develop my own identity as a minister."

As it happened, there were no synagogues available that wanted two rabbis, so Sandy and Dennis—the first rabbinical couple in the United States—had to take separate congregations. She became the spiritual leader of the Manhattan Reconstructionist Havurah, and he became a rabbi at the Reconstructionist Synagogue of the North Shore in Great Neck, New York.

"In the future I think we would consider taking a position together," she said. "Now that we're establishing ourselves independently, I don't think those other problems would occur. We view ourselves differently and other people would also be more likely to look on us as individuals."

But no matter how these ordained husbands and wives settle their ecclesiastical and theological differences, they face the same domestic problems that every working couple must resolve: Who's going to clean the toilet? Is it a man's job to vacuum the floors? Which spouse will cook and which will wash the dishes? Who will take the prime responsibility for the kids? These are very real problems because many of these ministerial couples can't afford a full-time maid.

Some women pastors, like Abigail Evans, have decided to mobilize their children: "I supervise all the work at home," she says. "Sometimes I like to think of myself as superwoman, but I'm not, so I divide the work load at home among my four boys. Vacuuming, emptying waste baskets, washing, doing the beds, cleaning the dishes, cooking breakfast—they do all these things. My job is to organize them."

For a while, her husband had only a short ride to his teaching job, so he was the one who took care of the boys. But now he has to travel farther, and the responsibility has fallen to Abigail.

A somewhat more traditional route has been chosen by Jean Arthur, the pastor of a United Methodist church in Derby, Connecticut. "I do think the man should be the head of the home—not the boss, but a final authority if there's a question," she said.

Her husband, Edwin, who runs a senior citizens center, said he believes a woman should be able to follow a career "as long as it doesn't interfere with her responsibilities, and that means the combined responsibility of the family—including the cooking and the cleaning, or the supervising of someone else to do these things."

Jean's exhausting Sunday schedule is a mixture of pastoral duties and housewifely chores. She gets up and puts a roast in the oven and then hurries to the church next door to conduct the worship service, preach and even sing in the choir. Then she returns to the parsonage to eat lunch with Edwin and their two children. Her son and daughter clean off the table and do the dishes as she rushes out again—this time to visit sick parishioners in the local hospitals. Jean's typical Sunday ends with a visit to an Alcoholics Anonymous group which meets weekly in her church basement.

An even more arduous set of domestic and professional duties plagues Linda Harter. Her four children are under five years of age, but she has chosen to take the prime responsibility for them and for all household chores. "Bill and I have discussed it, but we decided not to divide up home responsibilities," she said. "Bill has too many irons in the fire, not only with our parish but in continuing education for ministers in the field, theological education and Jewish-Christian affairs. Those duties take him to New York and other cities one weekend a month."

Although Linda's title is "associate pastor" and she receives only one penny a year as a salary—"because the parish contracted for only one minister's salary and the way we divide up the work is our business"—she actually functions as a full-fledged co-pastor. "The parish actually gets one and a half to one and three quarters ministers," she says wryly. "I'm on tap twenty-four hours a day for counseling, deaths or whatever comes up."

Linda prefers collecting her one penny and giving Bill top billing as pastor, even though he has tried to get her to assume a title that is more commensurate with her duties. "I don't want the responsibility that goes with the co-pastor's job on paper," she explained. "It's because of the pressure. On my typical day the little ones are up by seven, even though we sometimes don't go to bed before 1 A.M. After breakfast I have to do the kitchen cleanup. Then before noon I get in some church paper work. Then there's lunch, and around 2 or 2:30 P.M. the kids have their nap time. I may get some more work done then—maybe some counseling with a parishioner. I run household errands late in the afternoon, attend church meetings, make visits to the hospital. Then there's supper."

But this packed daily schedule provides "a constant source of tension," she admits. "Sometimes I feel frustrated that the little ones aren't getting enough attention. The frustrations are worse as we prepare for the Christian holidays because those are busy times for the church. I can't take the kids to see Santa every day during the Christmas holidays. Sometimes I really feel I'm being shortchanged, not being in the coffee klatches around here with the other mothers. They sit around and have coffee all morning, but my professional responsibilities keep me too busy. It can really aggravate me that I'm not free to join them. I know that what women talk about at the coffee groups is often pretty petty and doesn't involve much social concern. But it would be nice to be normal. I'd like to relax, not be professional, but it will never be that way."

After her third baby was born, Linda began to feel "resentment," and she decided "to have another baby and get out of it completely" —or at least for six months. But after she had been home for one week, after the birth of her fourth child, two people called to ask her to do weddings. "How can you turn them down?" she asks. "I really got mad that I couldn't get away from the ministerial role. But regardless of the way I tried to limit my duties, I found I just couldn't escape them."

Because she knew she couldn't take her frustrations out on the congregation, she said she took them out on Bill by getting snappy and argumentative.

"Why do I have to do this at all?" she asked him.

"Because you've been called to do it—called by your congregation and by God," he replied. "The people need you and God wants to use you."

"Big deal!" Linda said, but she sensed what he was saying was true.

Reflecting on that period of tension, she says with a smile, "I'm a great resister. I didn't want to accept my ministerial role—it was a continual battle. But now I'm into my job more than I ever was. I can't get out of it—I don't know how. People keep coming, wanting to talk to me. Bill keeps on slipping in a few weekends away. I don't know if I've resigned myself to being a pastor. But it would be easier if I just accepted my responsibility and did it. It's a case of a human being trying to escape God's will. Also, another reason I'm not out of the job is probably the fact that I don't want to be out of it. There's certainly something about it I do enjoy."

Some couples have found that a good way to relieve the double pressures of housework and pastoral duties that bear down on many married female pastors is for the husband to assume some of the domestic work. Rob and Arabella Meadows-Rogers have worked out an *ad hoc* arrangement, even though they first tried to plan all the housework down to the last detail.

"We originally envisioned a complex arrangement that would have taken an IBM computer to work out," Rob said dryly.

"It was my plan," Arabella pointed out. "Rob wanted to do it all by love!"

"Originally we were going to alternate every task in the house, but you'd have needed eighteen notebooks and forty-five columns," Rob said. "This would have met an organizational need of Arabella's, but not necessarily a functional one. What we do now is that we each take over the chores that are most important for us individually to have done. If I see dustballs in the corner, I get very uppity. I always like to have the floors clean. I think I do the floors better than Arabella, and I'm more concerned about getting into all the corners and vacuuming under the beds," he says with a wink. "I wouldn't have it any other way. I'd worry about the floors all the time, otherwise."

Rob's choice of the floor detail has gotten him into some interesting encounters in his church. An elderly woman called him one afternoon and said, "Pastor, can I talk to you for a moment?"

"Not really," he replied. "I'm in the middle of my floors."

"You're what?" the startled woman asked.

"I'm washing the floors," he explained.

"Oh, okay," she said and hung up.

But Rob realized, as he went back to his cleaning, that "it was pretty far from her consciousness that a male—much less a minister—

would be washing the kitchen floor. She seemed to think at first that for some reason I was *sitting* in the middle of the floor. Then she finally got it into her head that I was cleaning them."

Rob and Arabella's teamwork around the house became such a *cause célèbre* around the church that the church secretary gave them each an apron one Christmas. But despite Rob's successful and enthusiastic assumption of part of the housework, he still occasionally worries about his image. "I was vacuuming the floors one day after it got dark," he recalled. "The lights were on inside, and I suddenly realized that I could be seen from the street. I saw the mailman coming down the street, and I ran into the living room and the front hall and pulled down the shades so he wouldn't see me vacuuming the floors. I didn't want to hassle his stare. I'll discuss what I'm doing at home and joke around with the people in the congregation, but to have a strange person stare at me and wonder where my masculinity got lost for the past twenty-five years, that makes me quite nervous. I can laugh at that situation now, but it did make me uncomfortable."

If an ordained couple are so inclined, this teamwork approach can be applied not only to housework but also to ministerial responsibilities like counseling. Judy Hoehler and her husband, Harry, who is her co-pastor at a Unitarian church in Weston, Massachusetts, are particularly adept at working together to resolve problems of parents who have retarded children because one of their own children has this problem. On one occasion, for example, they were talking to a young mother and father who were upset about the fact that their new baby was mentally retarded. A physician asked the ministers to drop by the couple's home, and Judy opened the conversation by saying, "You know, we have a Down's syndrome child also, and I thought you might like to talk."

She then pulled out some pictures of her own child and the mother exclaimed, "Why, she looks normal! What's she doing riding a bicycle? They told me our child wouldn't be able to do anything."

"Doctors sometimes are misinformed," Harry replied.

"I guess so," said the father, who had even refused to look at his child up to this point.

"You know, it's very interesting what our child has done for us," Harry continued. "All of us who have gone through college and grad school tend to think that the main thing in life is the intellect and knowledge. But here is this child, whose capacity to give and receive love is as great as any of our other children. It's made us focus on the fact that maybe knowledge is not the most important thing. Here's a child who is in some respects the most open of our children. She's a great giver and receiver of affection and love. She sort of stabbed us awake, in other words, and made us realize we were putting the wrong priorities on our values."

In this counseling situation, Judy dealt with the problems of the wife and Harry addressed himself to the difficulties the man was facing. If either of them had been forced to work with the couple alone, the result would undoubtedly have been less effective. By the time the conversation was over, the young couple actually seemed to be looking forward to their experience as parents.

Sometimes this team counseling technique can provide the ordained wife with an opportunity to protect her husband, as well as help him advise parishioners. One male Methodist pastor in the Deep South had been approached after a church service by a voluptuous, thirtyish divorcee who told him she was having some problems with her former husband and wanted the minister's advice. She asked if it would be all right if she called him for an appointment, and he said, "Sure," and thought no more about the matter.

But the next day the woman phoned him at home and said, "I don't feel like coming over to your church office to talk about my problem because I haven't been feeling so good today. Do you think you could come over to my place this afternoon? It's really important."

Against his better judgment, the man agreed, but when he hung up the phone he turned to his wife and said, "I smell trouble. Why don't you go over there with me?"

Luckily, his wife was also an ordained minister who worked with him at the church, so her presence at such a counseling session would not have seemed unusual. When they arrived at the woman's apartment, the woman pastor's presence proved to be just what was needed. The female parishioner, expecting only the man, met them at the door in a transparent red negligee. On a coffee table in the living room behind her, there were a bottle of whiskey, two empty glasses and a bucket of ice. Soft, dreamy music was drifting out from the record player.

The parishioner swallowed hard, managed a weak smile and said, "Well, you know, by nature I'm a very affectionate person." She then invited them both in and tried to conjure up a personal problem so that their visit wouldn't be wasted.

Although a large proportion of pastor's husbands seem to be ordained ministers themselves, some husbands have had nothing to do with the ministry. But these unordained spouses can be just as helpful and supportive toward their wife's work as those with seminary training.

One pastor said that her husband—a professional educator—is "almost like a minister's wife. People like to have him at church functions, and he's good about fulfilling that role. He teaches Sunday school, too. But unlike the typical minister's wife, he clearly has an alternative to his church work. He has his own identity. I sometimes wish he would have supper ready when I get home or make cookies for people I invite in from the church, but he won't go quite that far. Still, he's good enough to serve guests for me sometimes."

White-haired Druecillar Fordham said that her husband, a carpenter who died several years ago, thought she was "crazy" when she first opened up her Baptist church in a Harlem storefront. But then he started coming regularly to hear her, and when she moved into a new building, he used his carpentry skills to fix the place up. "He was a Methodist, but after I started pastoring, he was baptized in my church and became a deacon," she said. "He did the majority of the work on the interior when we first moved into our present building, and he was a great singer himself—a great help to the church."

But sometimes it's impossible for a husband and wife to pursue separate careers and still be together regularly. Reverend Ruth Thompson's husband, Tom, started out as a preacher, but in mid-career he became a fund-raiser and had to travel a great deal and be away from home constantly. Ruth had been happy up to that point being a mother and minister's wife and helping with Christian education in Tom's churches. But then one evening he came home and told her about his plan to be interviewed for the highly mobile fund-raising job.

"I was very upset," she recalled. "I remember the day he went to the Parker House Hotel in Boston to have an interview with one of the company's vice-presidents. I told him, 'I don't even feel like pressing your trousers.' We had been so happy, and I couldn't picture what life was going to be like not being a minister's wife and not working together in the church. I said to him, 'I'll be praying all the time they won't like you at all.' "

But they did like him, and he was told he would have to move to Pittsburgh. Ruth was then confronted with a decision: "When I knew he was leaving the pastorate, I wasn't very comfortable with the idea of taking the kids out of school and moving down there"— especially since she knew he would be on the road most of the time anyhow. When Tom came home one weekend during his training period in Pittsburgh, Ruth said, "You know, I think I've got to volunteer for some kind of work somewhere, and I don't know what to do but church work."

He put her in touch with the First Baptist Church of Gardner, Massachusetts, and she's been the pastor there for the past twenty years.

"I felt strongly about my sense of call," she said. "One of us had to stay with the three children—the youngest was six then. It was obvious to both of us that I couldn't move around with him every two months. So now I save a month of my vacation in the winter in case he has a campaign in Florida at that time. He's managed to be assigned there for the past five years. Tom's good at his work, but as he grows older he hates being away so much. Since the children are gone now, it doesn't make much sense that we aren't together more."

When a woman chooses to become a pastor, it's inevitable that the very foundations of her marriage will be challenged, and the challenges come from every quarter. She may feel competition with her minister-husband. Or she may be driven to distraction by the tensions and sense of guilt that can accompany the joint responsibilities of household chores and pastoral duties. Or she may be torn apart emotionally by having to decide between following the call of God and supporting a husband's career.

But dealing with the man at home can be easy compared to overcoming the mystique of male authority that pervades the administrative structure of the local church and centers on the pulpit. It's at this point—as they gather up their robes and step up to claim the traditional throne of masculine spiritual authority—that the women are separated from the girls.

CHAPTER FIVE

The Masculine Mystique
of the Pulpit

As Ruth Thompson stood on the platform at the front of her Baptist church for the closing hymn of the church service, she was in a quandary about what to do. The silver-haired mother of three had never issued a Billy Graham-type altar call to urge members of her congregation to step forward and make a Christian commitment. But somehow she wanted to that morning.

Her congregation had experienced an uplifting lay witness program during the weekend, and she sensed they might want to express their deepening spiritual commitments publicly, but she just didn't know. "Don't rush through the hymn," she whispered to the organist. "I might want to do something different."

Her robe and nylon-lace white collar seemed especially warm, and she felt shaky and indecisive as they moved through the first stanza of "O Master, Let Me Walk with Thee." She swallowed hard as her mind raced with conflicting thoughts: "I don't know if I can get up enough courage. What will these people think? They may just die, and if no one comes forward, I may die too." There were well over a hundred people in those pews, and it seemed presumptuous to ask them to disregard their New England reserve and deeply ingrained traditions of worship.

But she overcame her reservations as something outside herself seemed to move her forward, uncertainly, down the steps of the platform to the front of the congregation. "After this weekend of being together, we've done some real deep sharing," she began. "I'm down here because, after what we've shared this weekend, I'm telling the Lord that I want to be a better communicator. I've failed to reach people; I've failed to open doors and go through them; and I'm telling the Lord I want to be better. If you want to come forward and stand here with me, then you will be saying the same thing."

There was a moment of stillness, and as they began the second stanza, Ruth heard a rustle behind her. She glanced back and noticed several members of the choir were moving out of their seats. As she looked back toward her congregation, she saw men, women, boys and girls edging their way to the aisles.

Ruth knew at that moment that God had indeed been leading her, so now she spoke more freely. "I'm concerned about a lot of things," she continued. "Some of our people have grown lukewarm, even cold, and as you know we have no one now to lead our young people. If you're willing to be used by the Lord, if you feel led to help us with our youth, this is the time to do something. And if you've never committed yourself to Christ, come, and we'll be happy to talk with you."

About forty people, including half the choir, were soon crowding around her at the front of the sanctuary. She spoke with many of them as they came forward, shook many hands. Five of the young adults said they had responded to her invitation because they wanted to help with the youth in the church. As Ruth gave the benediction from the front of the church, with so many members of her congregation crowding around her, she knew her church had reached a new spiritual plateau. And she could also be confident that she—or God through her—had exercised a public spiritual charisma that many male ministers aspire to, but few possess.

Despite the proven accomplishments of women preachers like Ruth Thompson, many people find they still have a built-in reluctance to accept the sight of a woman in the pulpit, a woman who stands before them as the symbol of spiritual authority in their church. There seems to be a masculine mystique surrounding the pulpit, a mystique which makes worshipers respond most readily to a booming, deep, authoritative voice and commanding presence.

Because women don't usually fit this image, they often find themselves facing a variety of arguments about why they should keep out of the pulpit.

Ruth herself is periodically barraged with the biblical passages on women keeping silence in the church. An auctioneer, who had been hired to sell some of her furniture as she was preparing to move into her Gardner, Massachusetts, parsonage, said, "So you're going over to Gardner as the Baptist pastor, huh?"

"Yes," she replied.

"What do you do with those verses that say women should be silent in the church?"

She gave her standard reply: "The Apostle Paul wasn't saying *every* woman has to be silent or subordinate. Throughout the New Testament he salutes women in leadership roles—Phoebe, Priscilla, Lydia. These women were pillars of the early churches." According to the New Testament, Phoebe was a deaconess in the church at Cenchreae (Romans 16:1); Priscilla helped teach the prominent male preacher Apollos proper Christian doctrines (Acts 18:26); and Lydia, a Macedonian businesswoman, turned her home into a headquarters and base of operations for Paul and other Christians (Acts 16:14–15, 40).

Ruth Thompson is not the only woman to have encountered biblical arguments against her preaching. Several disgruntled male ministers made an appointment with Southern Baptist minister Druecillar Fordham when she first opened her church in Harlem. One of the first things they did after they had taken seats was to cite I Corinthians 14:34–35 and argue "Paul said women should be silent in the church. The ministry isn't any place for a woman."

"If you believe that, you shouldn't allow women to teach or sing either," Druecillar said pointedly. "Things have changed. Paul made those statements to deal with a particular situation. Women were making a whole lot of noise in the church, and he told them to keep quiet."

There is substanial support for Druecillar's bibilical argument when Paul's first letter to the Corinthians is viewed as a whole. The verses in question, I Corinthians 14:33–35, read, "As in all the churches of the saints, the women should keep silence in the churches. For they are not permitted to speak, but should be subordinate, as even the law says. If there is anything they desire to know, let them ask their husbands at home. For it is shameful for a woman to speak in church."

But a few chapters before that in I Corinthians 11:5, Paul writes, ". . . a woman who prays or prophesies with her head unveiled dishonors her head . . ." The assumption in this passage is that women *are* permitted to speak in church, at least to pray and prophesy. In light of this passage, then, the internal consistency of the epistle can only be maintained if the silence verses in I Corinthians 14 are read to prohibit chattering during services or talking out of turn. This interpretation seems especially reasonable in light of a major theme that Paul stresses in the fourteenth chapter—that everything should be done in an orderly fashion during worship services. In fact, his sentence immediately preceding the silence passage is this: "For God is not a God of confusion but of peace" (I Corinthians 14:33). Undisciplined talking by anyone, male or female, would tend to disrupt this orderliness that he values so highly, and the talking problem at Corinth seemed to involve women more than men.

Some readers may also be bothered by the statement in I Corinthians 14:34 that women "should be subordinate, as even the law says." A few scholars dismiss this passage and the rest of verses 34–35 as a later insertion that was not part of the original Pauline text. But it seems possible to keep these verses and still maintain an internal consistency between chapters 11 and 14 if we ask, "To whom are the women supposed to be subordinate?" Paul answers that question for us in verse 35: they are to look to their husbands for guidance. The apostle seems to be relying here on the family units in the Corinthian church to correct the confusion caused by too much talking. He wants the husbands, who were the heads of their households, to exercise their authority and help restore order. The word "subordinate" thus refers to the woman's position in the family, not in the church community at large, where she may hold a responsible position that requires her to speak officially to the congregation.

A contemporary version of the situation in first-century Corinth may have been discovered by Jean Arthur while she was serving as a missionary in India. "I had a problem with Paul's ideas about women before I went over to India," she said. "But after I had arrived in India, I decided their culture is much like the Pauline culture must have been. In the churches over there, the women are uneducated.

The men and women are kept separate—as in some Jewish synagogues —and the women for the most part don't pay a bit of attention to what's going on in the service. I think the situation in Corinth was probably a lot like that. But remember, Paul just warned women to keep quiet as members of the congregation. He didn't tell them not to preach."

Even if the opponents of female pastors agree there are no biblical obstacles to putting a woman in the pulpit, some practical questions still remain: Can a woman be authoritative enough as she conducts worship services and dispenses the sacraments? Can she preach an inspiring, forceful sermon? Does she have the practical skills and business acumen to run a church?

When Joanne Whitcomb first took over as pastor of the United Methodist Church in Easthampton, Massachusetts, she sensed that the main resistance to her authority came from the lay women. One woman, in a rather hostile tone of voice, told her, "Women have more resistance to women ministers than to men." There seemed to be little doubt about the identity of the woman minister to whom she was referring. This message was confirmed during the first few weeks when a number of churchwomen seemed reluctant to shake Jo- anne's hand at the door after the sermon. "They wouldn't smile or look directly at me," she said. "They seemed very withdrawn. That attitude didn't last long after they got to know me, but I think some of them were afraid that their old comfortable stereotypes of male and female roles might be breaking down. They thought they knew who they were, but then I arrived and represented a threat. They didn't want to take on more responsibility. Also, for some of the women, it was just a feeling of jealousy."

Just as some women bridle at submitting to the spiritual leadership of a woman, some men also voice objections. Jean Arthur, a warm, motherly woman in her early fifties, found in her first pastorate that a group of about three men had decided they couldn't accept her in the pulpit. One of them even refused to shake her hand after the sermon every Sunday morning. And on more than one occasion she would hear him swear under his breath as he passed her, "This damned woman—thinks she knows it all!"

Another of the men kept a smile on his face but let her know he was waiting for her to make a slip: "You've never preached a sermon I can argue with yet, but I'm waiting," he said.

But after she had preached there for several months, she finally won them over. When she announced finally that she would be moving on to another parish, two of the men came up to her with tears in their eyes and asked if she couldn't stay for another year.

The constant need to prove herself in the pulpit has followed Jean into her present position as pastor of a United Methodist church in the industrial town of Derby, Connecticut. Her lay leader, Carroll "Chubby" Curtis, said that although at first some of the members "didn't think a woman could handle the job, she has proven she can do as good a job as a man. But to me it just doesn't seem the same having a woman minister in the pulpit. She's not as forceful in some respects."

Jean agrees that "in preaching, I think the man has the edge on the woman. I think a woman's forte is counseling."

She is not alone in her general opinion that women seem to have trouble projecting a forceful, commanding presence. Presbyterian preacher Abigail Evans says that she has found "a woman is much less of an authority figure in the pulpit." Although other women ministers disagree with these assessments, even the staunchest feminists admit there are some basic differences between the way men and women conduct themselves in front of their congregations during worship services and administrative meetings.

Joanne Whitcomb noticed one basic psychological difference between male and female pastors during an encounter that focused on her long, straight hair. Her tresses hung halfway down her back and kept falling over her eyes as she gestured to make points during her sermons. Her mother and several friends outside her church had suggested she cut her hair, and some people in the congregation made it a point to compliment her every time she rolled it up into a more compact coiffure.

Joanne finally chopped it off quite short, and as she was shaking her parishioners' hands at the door, several people raved about how nice she looked. But then an elderly lady, who always said exactly what she thought, leaned over and declared in a loud voice, "You looked like a witch before you cut it!"

Joanne laughed, but everyone else around her seemed rather embarrassed and hurried to get away. "It didn't bother me at all, but I'm sure most male ministers would have flipped out with her," she said. "As I thought about it, men pastors I've known tend to be much more defensive about criticism—their egos are more protected and they tend to lash out when something or someone from the outside attacks them. It's entirely a matter of ego. Women's egos don't have to go through the same process as a man's. Nothing is demanded of a woman as she's growing up. There are no demands that a female produce, but there are many demands with a male and this leads to a defensiveness which is a handicap for a minister."

Joanne, in other words, didn't feel that her image or authority were being threatened by her parishioner's straightforward comment. But when isolated comments turn into strident challenges to the pastor's spiritual leadership, maintaining control of the pulpit can get considerably more difficult.

With only brief experience in some rural parishes in upstate New York, Bonnie Jones-Goldstein found herself riding a whirlwind when she was assigned as pastor of the Washington Square Methodist Church in Manhattan's Greenwich Village during the height of the hippie movement. "I think they invited me to come because they were looking for a woman," she said. "It's the kind of church that always wants to do something different. I survived, but I was scared to death [when I went to that church]. I had no idea what to expect."

Bonnie's initial wariness about the church proved justified. She found in the first few weeks that Sunday attendance was as erratic as some of the individuals in her congregation. When she walked up to the pulpit, she never knew whether she would be speaking to five people or fifty, but she always knew there would be plenty of sweat shirts, blue jeans and uncombed heads. "There were kids who called themselves Communists in the church—they had rallies and parties to support China and Cuba. My husband, Steve, and I were the only married couple in the congregation. People lived together, but there were no other married couples."

The explicit challenges to her authority came from several directions. Although she had never been confronted personally with homosexuality before, one fellow walked up just after she had arrived and said, "My name is Sam and I'm a homosexual."

She stared at him for a moment and replied, "My name's Bonnie."

She didn't know what else to say, but Sam went on to tell her his entire life's story as a homosexual in New York City. Bonnie got the feeling throughout the monologue that he was implying, "Are you going to put me down, say I'm wrong?" He was probing her, challenging her to see if she would reject him or become judgmental about his activities. But she never did. The most that Bonnie would say to Sam and other homosexuals was, "I don't say you're wrong. At the same time I don't feel you're right. I don't see this in a moral dimension. I don't understand your perspective because it's not my perspective."

Her style was to avoid confrontations, to meet challenges indirectly in order to avoid dissension. Her non-committal, flexible stance on many issues was the complete antithesis of the traditional authority image that many male ministers try to project as leaders of the church. And the young people who were involved in radical politics sometimes seemed to try to push her as far as she would go. One group, who identified themselves as North Vietnamese Communists, insisted on hanging North Vietnamese flags on the front of the church on certain celebration days, and Bonnie offered no objections.

An atheist walked up to her after a sermon and said, "I don't believe in any of this religion stuff."

"Okay, I do, and if you come here you're going to be in a relationship with me," she replied.

"So what are you going to do about the fact that I don't believe there's a God?"

Instead of saying that her church existed only for those who affirm God and Christianity, she invited him to stick around and discuss the issue. "Probably a doctrinally rigid person would have been more threatened, because if you deny the God that makes you possible, who are you? But I didn't feel any of these challenges were subversive of my authority. I stated my own faith and convictions. I told him I believed in God. This fellow looked on Christ as a prophet and a good person, but I said Jesus means more than that to me. I said I believed in the Resurrection, and the physical resurrection makes him something more than just a man."

Bonnie was also unwilling to silence the young people in her congregation who wanted to comment during her worship services, so she set aside some time during each service for them to speak their minds on different issues. If she hadn't given them the time, they would probably have taken it, she noted.

Although most preachers are quite protective of their pulpits and insist on controlling who makes spiritual proclamations during services, Bonnie refused to assert her authority in that way. Despite some degree of disorder, one positive result was that she became more approachable to at least two young people who desperately needed her help. Ironically, both had been involved in religious communes which stressed truth and authority above all else. In other words, the environments from which they had come were almost the exact reverse of the loose style that Bonnie employed.

"One was a young woman who tried to kill herself in our church," Bonnie said. "She was on drugs, had taken an overdose of something. She came into the church to die." Apparently, it was the only place that she knew she could come, and she told Bonnie, "I want to die," and then passed out in front of her. Bonnie and some of the other people in the congregation rushed her off to a hospital and saved her life.

The other young girl was a homosexual. She had left her family and had moved into a religious commune, "but when they found out she was homosexual, they kicked her out," Bonnie said. "She had no support, no family, and it totally freaked her out. They rejected her completely. She had sought answers there. They had told her, 'We have all the answers for you.' But they didn't have the answer for her homosexuality. She could quote Scripture better than I could, but it didn't have any meaning for her."

Bonnie had this girl committed to a hospital so that she could receive psychiatric care. "There wouldn't have been any place for these two young women to go if we hadn't accepted them," she said. "This is a tension that I constantly live with—being open to others and not judgmental, and at the same time feeling the need to give a bold, straightforward presentation of the gospel."

Bonnie's experiences in the Greenwich Village church were more extreme than those encountered by most female preachers. But a large number of female pastors also seem to place a primary emphasis on being flexible on doctrine and approachable as human beings, rather than on being charismatic authority figures in the pulpit. Yet as non-judgmental as many women pastors seem to be, they demonstrate time and again that they can take unequivocal moral stands when the need arises.

Baptist Ruth Thompson gradually developed a sense of moral outrage about the Vietnam war, but some inner, unaggressive tendency in her personality kept her from speaking out for a long time. "Every Sunday I'd get ready to prepare a message, and I'd think 'I should be saying something, at least letting them know what it seems to me is right and wrong,'" she said.

One pastor whom she knew had refused to pay his income taxes one year to protest the war. When he was leaving his congregation to accept another post, she attended his farewell luncheon and pulled him aside for a chat. "If there's any one thing I've admired you for, it's that you've had the nerve to say and do what I haven't had the nerve to do," she said. "I've always looked up to you, and my heart has been with you marching in the streets."

But despite these sympathetic feelings, Ruth still found that she couldn't make herself take a public stand and run the risk of alienating members of her congregation. "I didn't have the nerve to attack the issue, at first," she said. "Other ministers I knew were being put out of their churches for taking a stand, but I kept quiet. Then I finally decided, 'I have to speak—not because my opinion is so important, but if I feel I'm an instrument of God, I have to speak on the hard things as well as on the easy things. I have no right to be the spiritual leader of people if I'm not going to give them some direction. A person who has been called to be the spokesman of God has to say something.'"

She sat down and prepared an anti-war sermon, and the next Sunday she got tough in the pulpit: "It's not important what my political views are," she told her congregation. "I'm talking about what the Word of God says, what the gist of it means to me. This is an immoral war. For example, I've heard at a recent church convention that the U. S. Navy has been purchasing tiger cages to imprison the North Vietnamese prisoners of war. This is wrong, and I think we Christians have to register our protest and stand up and be counted."

The teen-agers thought her sermon was great and immediately suggested that she preach on the same topic the next month. But she also made some enemies. One man, his face contorted in anger, walked up to her at the church door and said, "If I ever hear you talk like that again, I'm going to stand right up in the middle of the service and ask for equal time!"

"Oh no you're not!" Ruth retorted. "The pulpit is a place for proclamation by the minister. If we have a discussion about anything, we'll have it downstairs. We can talk about it as a group if you want, but not in the pulpit."

He stalked off without answering her, and she heard several other protests during the next couple of weeks. One family even left the church over the issue. But Ruth said, "I don't know of anything I've ever felt better about doing. I felt if anyone should be howling about an issue like this, it should be the church and Christian people."

Joanne Whitcomb chose a somewhat different way to express her opposition to the war to her Methodist congregation, but the reactions she received were almost as hostile. She got some pictures and slides, provided by an anti-war group, to demonstrate the anti-personnel weapons used in the air war. "I wanted people to be clear about what kind of war they were spending money on," she explained. "I toyed with the idea of having this program as part of the service, but some of the lay people I know said, 'When you have a captive audience like that, you're going to have trouble.' To me, it didn't seem that unfair, but I decided to show the slides after church so that they would be available on a volunteer basis."

She didn't say anything after the program had been presented, but when she turned the lights on, she could see "the people had started growling."

Two men confronted her and argued, "You should show the other side! You should present the other side! You're only showing one point of view!"

Joanne replied, "What do you mean? This is documented material taken from Air Force magazines and publicity handouts. It simply shows you what kind of weapons are being used. What other side is there? Sure, I suppose we could say our armed forces are going in there and giving money to people in hospitals after we've helped to blow their arms and legs off!"

Standing up for a moral principle sometimes involves more than just making pointed proclamations to a congregation, however. A few female pastors have found that the only effective way to make a prophetic point may be to become active in a movement, or in a street demonstration. Polly Laughland, the interim pastor of the Unitarian Society of Wellesley Hills, Massachusetts, decided she couldn't sit at home while she felt racial injustice was being perpetrated during the school busing violence in South Boston in the fall of 1974. She rode one of the buses herself, because, she said at the time, "I think the church should be present here as a witness to the fact that racial justice is a good thing."

When Polly described her experiences and feelings in a sermon to her parishioners, she found them to be quite interested and receptive. One said, "Thank you for doing this for us. It's not something we all can do."

She exhorted them from the pulpit by first pointing out her own inadequacies: "I grew up in Newton totally oblivious to black discrimination. I cringe to think of it and wonder now at our insensitivity." She concluded, "Could the power of love be enough to overcome the forces of fear and hatred? My optimism is at a low level."

Few would argue that the courage it sometimes takes to speak on a controversial topic or actually get involved in some sort of social action is a quality that women pastors have demonstrated as well as men. But what about the subtle powers of oratory? Can a woman present her sermons in such a way that she provokes tears, laughter or profound theological questioning among the members of her congregation?

When Susan Gertmenian stood up to give a Mother's Day sermon to her Afton, New York, congregation, she seemed to have several things against her. First of all, most of her eighty or so listeners were considerably older than she was. Also, even though she was married, she had no children, and that would seem a decided disadvantage on Mother's Day. To top off her drawbacks that morning, the topic she chose, the "motherhood of God," had a disturbingly feminist ring for a conservative blue-collar congregation.

But as she moved into her sermon, she could see that her listeners —especially the women—were hanging on her every word. Then she came to the main thrust of her message: "We're always depending on mothers to be ready to give, to be there to listen, to be ready to accept any burden that's laid on them. But mothers need mothers too. And God is a mother for those who have been bearing the burdens of others."

As Susan paused for effect, she saw that several people were wiping their eyes. One woman had been so touched that she was sobbing. "She had been bearing a heavy personal burden, and she really responded to what I was saying," Susan remembered. "I wasn't trying to make a feminist point. I really was thinking about several people who had been suffering when I prepared that sermon. The emphasis was on God as a parent, rather than on any particular sex."

Besides this ability to choose words that tug at the heart, women ministers are as capable as men in stimulating the minds of their congregations. Unitarian pastor Judy Hoehler, a forty-three-year-old who graduated at the head of her class at the Harvard Divinity School, considers herself to stand in the conservative, or "historical," tradition of Unitarianism. This means that even though she does not regard Jesus as God, she does believe he was "the messiah in terms of being the person who fully opened himself to the power of God. He became the channel of God's power for a broken world." Unlike the humanist or liberal wing of Unitarianism, however, she affirms the concept of God as a transcendent "center of personality with which we can relate in prayer."

With these theological assumptions guiding her, she frequently draws her sermon material from contemporary problems or events and then analyzes those problems in light of her faith. In one sermon, entitled "The Fractured Soul," she said she had received a fund-raising brochure in the mail from a women's college. On the front was a picture of a large red apple with a bite taken out of it. Next to the apple were these words: "Eve had the right idea."

Inside the brochure, on the first page, was this sentence: "Surrounded in Eden by an infinitely varied, deliciously fascinating environment, she rejected the haven of blissful ignorance and reached for knowledge—of herself and the world around her."

Many people—including, probably, quite a few male pastors—would have glanced at this brochure and tossed it aside without thinking about it. But Judy studied it, thought about it and realized that it "completely misunderstands the creation myths." With this ordinary, everyday starting point, she brought her biblical scholarship to bear on the problem and delivered a sermon in which she expounded upon the creation, the nature of man, the relationship between men and women and the reason for man's separation from God, his fellows and nature.

She noted that in the biblical context, the "knowledge" acquired by the partaking of the forbidden fruit was not an "abstract knowledge," as the college brochure seemed to imply. Rather, it referred to "knowing in the sense of becoming involved with." She also declared that the brochure erroneously assumed "the belief that knowledge heals—that with enough know-how we can solve the world's ills and bring in the harmony of a new Eden."

Judy's conclusion went in part like this: "A sober look at history reminds us that knowledge does not overcome brokenness. The best-educated nation of its time produced Dachau. The most literate country in the world dropped the first atomic bomb. So knowledge is not enough. The biblical witness points in another direction. Not knowledge alone, but faithful service to a gracious Lord who calls us to live for one another—that is what heals."

These are serious, thought-provoking words, but female ministers in the pulpit can also rival some stand-up comics. Another Unitarian minister, Polly Laughland, decided that things too often bordered on the lugubrious in her worship services, so she put together a "funny service" for her Wellesley Hills congregation. She got her male religious education director and a female student minister to stage a skit involving the comic-strip characters from *Peanuts*, Charlie Brown and Lucy. She also read a James Thurber fable and had her congregation sing altered words for some traditional hymns.

Although some traditional Christians might find a few of these hymns offensive or even sacrilegious, Polly comes out of the liberal non-theistic humanist Unitarian tradition, so her humor was more successful in her church than it might have been elsewhere. In one case, alterations were made in the familiar hymn which begins, "Holy, Holy, Holy, Lord God Almighty . . ." The changed version, written by Christopher G. Raible, read, "Coffee, coffee, coffee, praise the strength of coffee. Early in the morn we rise with thought of only thee. Served fresh or reheated, dark by thee defeated, brewed black by perk or drip or instantly."

"Coffee is sort of our Unitarian Communion," Polly explained. "People get together in Unitarian churches around the coffeepot. There's usually not a Communion service."

Although the service provoked a number of broad grins and chuckles, Polly stressed that "there was a serious intention. Laughing is part of the whole of life. If religion is concerned with wholeness, then laughter should be okay in church."

Using an equally creative approach to worship, Bonnie Jones-Goldstein began to experiment with modern dance in the sanctuary when she was in college and seminary. She continued to choreograph some parts of her services after she became pastor of the unconventional Washington Square United Methodist Church in Greenwich Village. "I do interpretations of Scripture and church music by dancing myself and organizing groups of dancers," she said. "The dance has helped me see that worship is more than intellectual. I can understand the Scriptures in a physical, feeling way."

On one occasion, she did a Christmas dance program which revolved around an interpretation of Mary, the mother of Christ. A group of female dancers performed at the foot of a cross and concentrated on "inward, downward stuff, holding onto each other. There was not much leaping. They tried to express their relationships with other women."

Probably few conventional churchgoers can imagine a male minister dancing around on the platform in front of the sanctuary or conducting a "funny service." Some might even argue that such activities are undignified or perhaps even degrading to a place which is supposed to inspire reverence and respect. But there can be no denying that women ministers have demonstrated that they are creative and imaginative in developing new forms of worship, as well as competent in preaching traditional sermons. But until the skills of the growing ranks of female ministers become generally recognized in the churchgoing community, women preachers will probably find, as Methodist pastor Norma Rust has observed, that "there is a subtle but very real resistance to women in the pulpit. Because you're a woman, you may not be accepted even though you have all sorts of abilities. I feel that in order to remain in the ministry, I'll have to do a caliber of work that's above what a man has to do. For a woman to be accepted, she has to be a step above a man. And I see myself as responsible not only for my own accomplishments, but also for all the other women who are coming into the field. Our work is being scrutinized very closely, and if we fall flat, people will say, 'That's what happens when you have a woman in the pulpit.' If I fail, in other words, I'm letting down all those who come after me."

The pressure on women pastors to measure up to the masculine mystique of the pulpit spills over into other traditionally male pastoral functions. Many men ministers, for example, become experts as handymen, electricians and plumbers because of the constant demands of the physical plant they oversee. But women are generally regarded as inept in these areas.

When Norma Rust, a widow, first became pastor of a church in Connecticut, she found that some of the male church leaders would get involved in long conversations about electrical wiring, heating, construction and other difficulties in the church. The problem was that they mostly talked and didn't act. "They assumed it would all be Greek to me," she said with a smile.

What the men had not counted on was the fact that before her husband had died, Norma had worked in a hardware store. "I was very much aware of what they were talking about because I had been involved in these things," she said. "I had worked with contractors and was accustomed to hearing about wiring and heating."

One evening, she finally decided she had heard enough. "Now you've talked about this and that and the other thing," she told them. "But you are leaders and have a responsibility as stewards of this church, and our congregation expects things to happen."

Without knowing her hardware store background, one man made some comment about how hard it was to choose between several complex types of locks for one of the doors. "I told him which locks were wrong and which were right, and that kind of took them aback," she recalled.

"How do you know about these kinds of locks?" the man asked.

"I worked with them in a hardware store before I became a pastor," she said.

"Well, okay, but it does take some lengthy discussion to decide about building the church parking lot," another man interjected, apparently attempting to test her knowledge further. "We have to decide how to process the gravel, how it should be cared for, when it should be oiled . . ."

What he didn't know was that Norma's husband had spent years in just this kind of work. "He was a road builder, and I heard about

processing gravel and caring for it night after night after night."
When Norma began to display her expertise in this area, the men
were convinced.

"From then on, things happened," she said. "Doors on the church
were chained properly to meet emergency regulations, the downstairs
was painted, the parking lot was fixed, the fence was repaired, the
lights were fixed. A whole lot of things they had been talking about
actually began to happen."

But what if a tough physical challenge confronts the woman who is
working alone at night in her church? What if a loud drunk starts
pounding on her door, or if a burglar gets inside the building? Does it
take a man to handle that situation?

Baptist pastor Druecillar Fordham was confronted with a frightening challenge one day in her Harlem church, which is located in a
four-story brownstone on a block packed with a dozen other similar
churches. She was working in her study, and she heard someone
shuffling around behind a locked door next to her. She rushed over to
the door and called, "Who is it? Who's there?"

"Missus, I got mixed up on my room," a deep male voice came
back. "Could you open the door and let me back outside?"

"Just a minute," Druecillar said. She realized he could only have
entered that room through the roof from one of the adjoining brown-
stones, so she tiptoed into another room and dialed the police.

The man, apparently realizing what she was doing, rushed to a narrow staircase in an effort to get to the basement level and crawl out,
but he found the windows boarded up and all the doors locked.

"He started whooping and hollering something terrible," Druecillar
said. "There wasn't a soul downstairs but him, and he was banging on
the door and creating a stir in the street outside."

A young man, who had just driven up outside in a station wagon,
heard the noise and saw Druecillar looking out of her window for the
police. "What's wrong in there?" he shouted up.

"There's a man in here and he's trying to get out," she called back.

The young fellow ran downstairs to the door which the would-be
burglar was trying to break down. Just as he got there, "the man
busted the door down and busted his head open and hurt his leg,"
Druecillar said. "The boy caught hold of him, and by this time the

cops were coming from both ends of the street. They had to take the guy to the hospital before they took him to jail."

In a completely different setting, Presbyterian preacher Abigail Evans found that almost as much courage and initiative were required when she took on the physically demanding job of being a circuit-riding preacher in the hill country of eastern Kentucky. For two years, Abigail, her blond hair whipping in the breeze, drove her Volkswagen miles and miles over the "stomping grounds" of the Hatfields and the McCoys: "the hilliest, narrowest, most treacherous roads I've ever seen in my life," she said. "The shoulders of the roads would disappear over the sheer edge of a cliff. When I arrived at a church, I was glad to be there in one piece, and the people were just as glad to see me. They were happy to see anybody who took an interest in them, or who was new or the least bit interesting. You might wonder, 'How could they accept a woman?' But it was a people-oriented culture."

No one objected to her preaching on the ground that she was a woman. Nor did anyone throw scriptural passages up to her about women being silent in the church. Instead, she encountered a friendly curiosity: "Out of all the supply preachers we've ever had, you're the first woman," one man said.

Her congregation consisted of thirty or forty people, most of them strip miners. Some wore the only suits they owned to church—often crumpled, old-fashioned blue serge outfits. Other men wore khaki pants and wool shirts. "These men and women had a certain dignity," she said. "Their English is really old English, with a lilting quality to many of their phrases. They're not outgoing—very reserved. And there was a slight stoop to the body in many of them—especially the coal miners who were unemployed. Sometimes I sensed that the spirit had died in the person. You have people down there who look a lot older than their years—men in their forties who look as though they're in their sixties, with deep creases and furrows in their faces."

No matter how much ability women preachers show in handling emotional and physical challenges, the pastoral headache which is often most difficult to remedy centers on the struggle with the lay leaders for administrative control of the congregation. The policy of certain congregations dictates that some pastors have more administrative authority than others. But there is a gray area in every church's power structure—a battleground on which a strong preacher can fight to increase control over church administration and finances. The less aggressive preacher, who refuses to take up the gauntlet of powerful lay people, may become limited to a role as spiritual, rather than administrative, leader of the congregation.

Diane Pierce, the young Congregational pastor from Connecticut, says, "I leave the business of the church up to the men. If the men don't do it, it doesn't get done because I don't do it. If they ask me to do what I consider to be their work, I just say, 'That's for the men.' I tell them my only reason for being here is to stand up for the Lord— to speak, bring the people closer to God, oversee their spiritual welfare. Other than that, I have no authority in the church at all."

Methodist Jean Arthur has found that the tradition of lay leadership in her church prevents her from wielding administrative or financial power: "You don't really govern because the trustees rather than the pastor here have run things for so many years. I don't get a sense of power unless God speaks through me. If I feel authoritative, I know it's God, not me. Although some women are dogmatic in their approach to church authority, I think that's more a male than a female characteristic."

In her dealings with the lay leaders in her church, Joanne Whitcomb finds that when she expresses an opinion, "they don't interrupt me, but they often don't agree. They're not rude, but they do discount what I say. For example, they couldn't care less whether I come to the meetings of the trustees. They never call me to remind me of the trustees' meetings. Probably it's the idea that a woman doesn't understand business matters."

The experiences of these women provide an interesting answer to those who would argue against women preachers by relying on the Apostle Paul's statement in I Timothy 2:12, "I permit no woman . . . to have authority over men." The experiences of the Reverends Pierce, Arthur and Whitcomb would indicate that a person can be a pastor and preacher without having to exercise "authority over men" in the administrative sense. A preacher, male or female, can proclaim the gospel message from the pulpit, in other words, and still leave the financial and organizational leadership to the laity.

But even if lay people retain the reins of administrative authority in a church, they sometimes get embroiled in internal controversies that have allowed female pastors to demonstrate a power to negotiate and reconcile that would do justice to a skilled diplomat. Margaret Frerichs has served as interim pastor for several Congregational churches which have confronted such dissensions, and she believes that "the fact that I was a woman may have been especially helpful. A woman can be more tactful and gentle. She exercises a reconciling function—that's a good way to describe it."

In some churches where Margaret has served, the previous minister had a strong personality and polarized the congregation: "Some responded positively to him, others didn't respond. When the minister left, you had two factions: the people in the church who worshiped the minister felt that no one else could ever replace him, but the other group was glad to see him go. If a permanent minister, rather than an interim pastor, follows this controversial pastor, this new, permanent person is likely to fall into the same pattern. People who didn't like the old minister will rally around the new one, and those who did like him will fall away. And you'll have the same two groups again."

But when an interim minister comes in before the next permanent minister, the situation may be different, especially if that interim pastor is a woman like Margaret Frerichs. "I wasn't as likely to draw those opposing responses," she explained. "People didn't have to make up their minds whether they liked me or not because I wasn't permanent. I often sensed I was in a tense situation, but it was more acceptable for me, as a woman, to act gentle and tender. If a man acts that way, people might object that he's not being forthright."

Her technique as an interim pastor was to call on key parishioners and ask those from the different factions what they thought of the situation in the church. But she let them know she cared for them as individuals, rather than as members of conflicting groups: "I told them the factions made no difference to me, and I tried to make them look toward the broader spiritual and social goals of the church and get their minds off the conflicting personalities."

Sometimes women pastors are so opposed to creating dissension in a church that they demonstrate a degree of patience that would do credit to Job. Reverend Ruth Thompson has noted that "the Baptist clergy don't have much authority, according to the letter of the law." Bowing to this denominational tradition, she has sometimes chosen to take a rather passive, unaggressive stance when a controversial issue involving church business arises. When she first took over her American Baptist pastorate there was a great deal of discussion about putting up an addition to the main building. "We had an architect in the church who had done a number of government and school buildings," she said. "He drew up the first couple of plans, but they didn't please everybody. Well, we were over a barrel. If we refused his plans, we would alienate a church family. But if we took them, we would be spending thousands of dollars for something many people didn't want."

Instead of pushing the issue, Ruth convinced the church leaders to wait. "My husband would come home from one of his fund-raising trips and say, 'Did you get the thing moving yet?' But I told him no, because there was a line down the middle of the fellowship on the building. The older folks would have gone along with it, but the younger ones wanted something else. If we had gone ahead, it would have split the congregation right down the middle. A man might have gone ahead and pushed the thing, but he would have spent the next ten years healing the hurt and mending the wounds."

With some gentle pressure from Ruth, the congregation decided to wait—for a total of ten years. "It was good, in a way, because we accumulated about $56,000." Also, the old plans had by then become a dead issue. The church leaders hired another architect, who presented a plan that was acceptable to everyone. "It worked out fine, and we gave the first architect some money to say thank you," Ruth noted.

Her technique for handling this potentially explosive administrative problem demonstrates what she regards as a "feminine quality" in the pastorate. "I used to say when I first came here that every Baptist church that has a problem should have a woman for one or two years to get things quieted down. There is more of a tendency toward gentleness and patience in a woman than in a man. A quality of motherhood or something is more evident in the female preacher."

But not every female pastor is willing to wait ten years in order to avoid a fight. Reverend Norma Rust had been working with several lay leaders in one Methodist church to try to straighten out a number of complex items in the annual budget. Some members in the church didn't like the budget, however, and without Norma's knowledge they called a meeting of a few members of the Administrative Board—the governing body of the church—and rejected the budget.

Just as Norma was preparing to walk up into the pulpit the next Sunday morning, one of the people who had set up the meeting called her aside and said, "Thursday night at the administrative board meeting, we decided we're not going to accept the budget."

"Thursday night?" Norma replied in surprise. "Administrative board? Who called an administrative board meeting for last Thursday night?"

"Oh, a few of us did."

Norma usually tries to walk into the service with a feeling of being "calm, peaceful, full of the Spirit of God, ready to help others. But boy, at that point I was ready to go through the roof. I was so angry I figured it was better to keep quiet until I was able to collect myself. But after I proceeded through the service and got to the point where announcements are made, I said there would be another board meeting on Monday night."

She spent most of Sunday night calling the members of the board to be sure they were all there this time. At the Monday night meeting, she laid her feelings out in the open: "You can't operate like this because that other meeting was irregular, and improperly called! You didn't follow the Methodist Conference rules."

After a few minutes of heated argument, the rebellious board members saw it her way. But Norma has reservations about getting embroiled in such arguments. "I'm uptight about confrontations like that—I just don't like them," she said. "But by the same token, I'm very much aware of where I am insofar as my responsibilities to the church are concerned. I know what I have to do to help the poor guy or woman who follows me. Any precedent I set will probably be carried on. If I allowed some of these people to get by with pushing me around, heaven help the pastor who follows me."

Reverend Linda Harter took a similarly firm stand when she ran into some problems while serving as "moderator" in a Presbyterian church which was temporarily without a pastor. The male leaders at the church's business meetings needled her about the fact that she was a woman, but she refused to let them put her on the defensive. In fact, she went on the offensive and set a new precedent for service as a church moderator: "These churches have to pay your travel expenses, but I decided to charge them with baby-sitting expenses too," she recalled with a smug smile. "The presbytery backed me up, but just to show they wouldn't completely accept the idea, these church leaders insisted on holding their meeting and another church's meeting on the same night so that they wouldn't have to foot the entire baby-sitting bill."

As women pastors pour out of American seminaries in greater numbers, they are bound to find resistance as they take over the nation's pulpits and raise their voices in the administrative bodies which are often the real repositories of ecclesiastical power. But the groundwork is being laid for the acceptance of these women preachers as sympathetic congregations and male preachers help remove the obstacles in their paths. The Park Avenue Methodist Church on Manhattan's Upper East Side is a case in point. Lay women there have rotated in and out of such positions of responsibility as chairperson of the Administrative Board, chairperson of the Council on Ministries (the Board's executive committee) and members of the church's powerful board of trustees.

The Park Avenue pastor, Reverend Philip Clarke, decided to throw the last bastion of masculine tradition completely to the winds when he accepted a suggestion by Janice Harayda, one of the church's lay women, that all the sex roles in the worship service should be reversed one Sunday. One of the female members of the congregation, Theressa Hoover, who is also a high official in the United Methodist Church, agreed to give the sermon. Other lay women served as ushers and helped lead the prayers and read the Scriptures.

The upside-down service culminated during the post-worship coffee hour. The church's women had always handled these refreshment tasks in the past, so many visitors did a double-take when they read through the church bulletin and saw this notice: "Coffee and tea will be served in Fellowship Hall after the service. Members and friends are invited to share in these moments of warmth made possible for us today by Mr. Bates, Mr. DeSear, Mr. Guise, Mr. Heaton, Mr. Hughes, Mr. James, Mr. Sieg and Mr. Taylor."

The service gained wide, favorable publicity in both the New York *Times* and the *Daily News*, and undoubtedly planted the seed of the same idea in the minds of other lay people and pastors. As steps of this type are taken by other congregations, the masculine mystique of the pulpit will inevitably disappear and be replaced with a greater sense of openness and approachability, without regard to the pastor's sex. Reverend Philip Clarke observed that the unusual Park Avenue service "was in keeping with the liberating spirit of the historic time in which we live. The women of this parish have far-ranging abilities and serve the church in many ways. We are grateful for their many contributions of time, talent and energy. We hope there will be other occasions of this nature in the months to come."

If such churches begin to introduce women as participants in their worship services on a regular basis, the acceptance of female pastors in the pulpit may become as easy as accepting cookies from the ladies during the coffee hour.

CHAPTER SIX

The Open Woman

A middle-aged man who had recently lost his wife was trying to adjust to becoming both mother and father to his children. A female pastor who had been widowed herself decided that, as his minister, she should check up on him occasionally to see how he was getting along.

"Are you having any problems with the cooking?" she asked him one afternoon at his home.

"No, no, the kids are helping me with that," he replied. "But you know, I really want to get married again. It's too hard for a single man my age with a family to try to make it alone. As a matter of fact, I'm already going rather seriously with a woman."

"Why, that's great!" the minister exclaimed. She decided that his situation was working out well enough for her to be able to cut down on her visits.

But then she heard through the grapevine that things had gone sour in the man's budding love affair. "The whole thing fell apart, and he was all upset," she recalled. "The next thing I knew he was knocking on my door, telling me the sad story."

They discussed the problem for a while, and just as the man got up to leave, he surprised the pastor by asking, "By the way, would you like to go out to supper tonight?"

"No, not really," she said candidly.

He smiled, shrugged his shoulders and left, but he kept dropping over to visit her—usually just when she got home from work at suppertime. He offered again to take her out to eat, but she still turned him down. Finally he came out with what was really on his mind: "I'd be interested in dating you with thoughts of getting married."

"That's fine, but I'm not interested," she said. "You're a nice guy, but I have other problems and other things in mind. I'm in no way interested in you or anybody else at this time. I've just barely gotten into this profession and I have a lot at stake. I'm not about to give it up at this point, that quickly."

But her suitor kept persisting. "He came back a couple of weeks later with the same tale," she said. " 'I'm having trouble with the kids, having trouble here and there, how about a movie?' "

"I'm really not interested," she told him bluntly. "If that's why you're coming here, you ought to cut it out. I'll be glad to help you in any other way, but I'm not at all interested in dating or marriage."

Finally, the man gave up, but she managed to keep on amiable terms with him. This experience suggests that a close connection exists between a woman preacher's expressions of warmth and concern for others and her basic sexual identity as a female.

"There's an innate feminine ability to care and be open, a maternal instinct to reconcile and give to others," declared pastor Abigail Evans. "A woman has to open up for there to be a sexual relationship, and this physical need is reflected in the very essence of our beings. I don't think it's incidental that God made the male and female the way he did."

The experiences of female pastors in counseling and other personal encounters bear out the basic truth of Abigail's observation: many female preachers *do* seem to be endowed with certain distinctive personality traits, such as approachability, openness and a maternal instinct to care and create harmony. These characteristics can enhance their performance of pastoral duties, and also can get them into hot water when their warmth is misinterpreted by male parishioners as either weakness or sexual availability.

A classic example of how parishioners can respond to maternal, pastoral characteristics is Southern Baptist minister Druecillar Fordham. Nearly everyone in her Harlem neighborhood calls her "Mother" Fordham, and the relationships she has developed with many of the local young people qualify her quite well for this title.

A specialist in family relationships, she believes that one of the main problems with young people today is that they are not as committed to school or to moral principles as they should be. But as an objective kind of surrogate parent, she gets annoyed when the real parents put all the blame on the kids. "When I talk to kids about dropping out of school, I always pray with them about it. I listen to the child's story and then I go to the parents. Two thirds of the time, it's the parents' fault, not the child's. It all starts in the home. Parents tell their children, 'Don't lie about this, always tell the truth about that.' Then when the phone rings, they tell their child, 'Tell them I'm not home.' These parents are training their children to lie. The adult problem is one of the biggest problems of the day. We talk about teen-age drop-outs, but it's the adult drop-out that's the big problem— parents who don't live up to their responsibilities."

The parents in her church talked her into preaching one Sunday on kids dropping out of school, but she turned the tables on them and spoke on this adult drop-out theory of hers. "Drop out of church, drop out of activities, drop out of the community," she told her congregation. "If something is wrong at school, the parents won't go there and find out the problem and correct it.

"A woman who lives near here once told me, 'I send my child to church every Sunday, but he never goes.' I asked, 'What about you— do you go?' She answered, 'I need to take my rest.' I said, 'Why don't you get up and bring him?' She said, 'Well, I'm so tired.'"

The children came for this service and drank in every word. The parents—some of them a little embarrassed—told her afterward, "Well, you have a point. We hadn't thought about it quite like that."

Mother Fordham also keeps her office and parsonage doors open for any young people who want to talk their problems over with her. She's especially interested in making inroads into solving the drug problems which for years have plagued the black community in New York City.

"It's pretty tough, the drug problem," she says, squinting her eyes thoughtfully. "I think I can put my hand on three fellows now that we don't have any trouble with any more, though. I sat down and talked with them, but I found I had to keep watch over them. So I appointed church people to keep an eye on each of them, call them, ask them over for dinner and discussions.

"There's one block near here where most of the drug traffic originates," she said. "It's so sad—sometimes I go down there and eat my heart out. I try to talk to the young addicts on that street, but I can't get through to them sometimes. When they listen, I let them know I know they're human beings and I love them. We had one of those young men join our church. It was great when he walked up and gave me his hand—I took it and prayed for him. It's important to show them somebody cares. But it takes a lot of time. You've got to have a lot of patience."

Mother Fordham, an expert at reconciliation, also has tried to smooth over racial tensions in her community. She had a number of long discussions with a man who was involved in a militant group and had developed some anti-white attitudes.

"Trying to fight the white man won't get you anywhere," she told him.

"God is black!" he shouted angrily.

"God is spirit," she replied. "God doesn't have any color. And fighting whitey won't help you either. When you go downtown tomorrow, who's going to give you your job? Do you have enough blacks to supply all the jobs? Before you start to fighting whitey, you'd better think it over two or three times. You have to learn God has promised to supply your every need, but he didn't say whether it would be by blacks or whites."

After a series of such discussions, she said, "He came around. He saw it my way."

Druecillar Fordham's efforts over several decades to reconcile the old and the young, the black and the white in her community have reinforced her maternal image in her church. Other female pastors, even if they're not dubbed "Mother" by their congregations, have found that they have assumed similar roles with their parishioners.

"When people come to me for counseling, sometimes they act like little children," observes Bonnie Jones-Goldstein. "They say, 'I hurt, I have a problem in my marriage, and I want you to make my hurt feel better.' Men especially tend to be more childlike with me. Women are more standoffish at first, and they want to be in more of a peer relationship than a counseling relationship."

But some pastors have found that women relate better to a woman counselor than to a man. Judy Hoehler has learned in her Unitarian congregation that the fact that she is a mother and a professional woman encourages other working mothers with vocational questions to seek her out.

"Some of the women I see are conscientious mothers as well as professional women," she explained. "Their concern is often how to provide emotional support for their children and at the same time carve out for themselves a place in life. They ask, 'How important is it to be home when your child comes home from school?' I've always felt it was important, but my usual approach is to be non-directive as long as I can. Still, they expect to hear some things from me since I'm a professional counselor. I'm not reluctant to say what I think, but sometimes they just want to talk about the problem."

Sex is another issue that many women prefer to discuss with another female. In one conservative rural community in the Midwest, for example, a mother overcame her innate reluctance to talk about sex and told her woman pastor that she was suspicious that her daughter was a lesbian.

"Some of her teachers at school have suggested this to me, so I think it must be true, but I don't know what to do."

"Have you talked to your daughter?" the minister asked.

"No, we never talk about sex. Never have been able to."

"How about your husband?"

"Are you kidding?" the woman replied. "My daughter would never talk to a man about this. Besides, I don't think a man could begin to understand."

"Do you want me to talk with your daughter?"

"Oh, yes, would you? I was hoping you'd see her. I think she'll come over here, and I'm sure she'd say more to you than she will to me."

This woman pastor found the girl to be a lesbian, but also "a very rebellious kid on the surface—an 'I don't need anybody' kind of person. She's opened up quite a bit in the sessions we've had together. But she's not so open that she wants to communicate with her parents—at least not at this stage. I'm the one who has to keep working with her."

Another very difficult problem for some women to discuss with a male pastor is infertility. A female pastor from the South had a visit from a woman who had been trying unsuccessfully for more than a year to have a baby, and she felt that her sex life and her entire married life as well were beginning to crumble around her.

"I'm so worried, I don't think I'll ever be able to provide my husband with a child," the parishioner said.

"Do you have a doctor that you're consulting regularly?" the pastor asked.

"Oh, yes. And he told us we're most likely to conceive in a twenty-four hour period right in the middle of the month. But everything is becoming distorted. Our entire sex life is so mechanical. My husband stays away from me before my fertile period—saves himself, you know. Then we're in bed all the time in those twenty-four hours. Our bedroom has become kind of like a stud farm or something. What pleasure is there in that? I've really started hitting bottom every month when my period comes and I realize we've failed again."

"Have you consulted a fertility expert?"

"What's that?"

The pastor explained that there are medical specialists who could conduct other tests to determine whether there was some obscure problem which might have escaped them.

"But you have to approach this thing very objectively—try every possibility and make up your mind you won't get discouraged," the minister said. "And above all, you must learn to trust God from day to day. You believe there's a God who acts in our lives—that's the reason you came to me instead of to a secular counselor. He'll give you the grace you need to cope with this problem if you'll just learn to trust him."

One of the most distasteful problems that a minister may face confronted a pastor who was having a casual chat with a young teenage girl in her congregation. The girl's family were regular churchgoers and seemed to have most of their problems under control, but the minister sensed that something was gnawing at the youngster.

"What's the matter?" the preacher asked. "Something bothering you?"

"Not really, but there's something I haven't told anybody outside our family, and I wanted to know what you thought about it."

"What's that?"

"Well, it's not a problem now, not at all. But my father tried to have sex relations with me last summer."

The young pastor almost tipped over in her chair, and she got very angry, "but I tried to maintain some level of calm," she said. "I'm sure I must have looked concerned, but the girl didn't seem too upset."

"We took care of it, though," the girl continued. "My dad said that he knew he was wrong and that he should see a psychiatrist."

"Did he?"

"Yes."

This minister wanted to be sure that the situation at home was under control so she asked a couple of key questions: "Did you go and talk to your mother about this?"

"Oh, yes. I told her right away."

"Well, I'm glad you did that. It's important to bring things like that right out into the open immediately. Now tell me. Do you feel comfortable with your father? Do you have any sense this might happen again?"

The girl assured the preacher that the problem seemed resolved and was sufficiently in the open in the family to put everyone on guard in case there was any inclination for her father to misbehave again. The minister acted as a sounding board to reassure the girl that she had been morally correct in rejecting her father's advances and notifying her mother about his conduct. Also, the pastor helped reinforce the girl's notion that under no circumstances should such improper conduct be tolerated again. In retrospect, this minister concluded that, where the offender is a father figure, it is probably easier for the girl to seek out a mother figure—a woman pastor—for moral advice, rather than another father figure.

But women and girls are not the only ones who prefer to come to a female pastor with their problems. Some men are also drawn by the maternal image that many female pastors project. Reverend Margaret Frerichs, who has served as pastor of several Congregational parishes, opened her parsonage door one day and found a young man from her church standing there. His face was creased with worry that would have been more appropriate for someone years older.

"What's the problem?" she asked as she ushered him into her study.

"Something's been bothering me for several months now, and I decided I'd better talk to somebody," he replied, taking a seat. "You're the only person I felt might be able to understand. You know, I just realized that I'd be worth more to my family dead than alive."

"What do you mean?" she asked.

"Well, I'm making a good salary, in a good position, but I've got a lot of insurance. If I should die—or be killed—that insurance would give my family more than I can give them now."

"What are you saying?"

"Suicide," he blurted. "I've actually been thinking about that as an option."

"But you have so much to live for!" Margaret cried.

"Do I really?" he replied dejectedly. "I've been wondering what life is really all about, whether it's really worth living. Even though I've got a good job, I don't think what I'm doing has much meaning."

"But you don't really think suicide is an answer, do you?"

"Probably not," he sighed. "But you see, I think it might be God's will for me to go into some sort of full-time social work or something like that. That way, I could give myself more to people's real needs, rather than just satisfy my own economic desires. But I can't do that. There's my family. If I started all over again, my personal finances would be much worse. I'm locked in, so I find myself wondering, 'Why not just end it all?' "

"Well, I think you know that's not an acceptable solution," she said. "But maybe you're not really examining all the possibilities. I agree with you that, given your family situation, it would probably not be a good idea for you to give up everything and enter a life of service. For some people, that might be the answer, but I don't think you'd be satisfied with that. You may expect me to be idealistic about this sort of thing, to tell you to give up everything, but I always try to be realistic. We all have to make adjustments and compromise so that we don't allow our desire for personal satisfaction to overshadow our commitments to others. What God wants you to do with your life is bound up with what's best for both you and your family. That means weighing abilities and talents and the total environment of your life— trying to work out what's best for everybody."

During several lengthy counseling sessions, Margaret and this man explored all the alternatives and he finally decided that he would continue in his same job but devote all his spare time to volunteer work. He found that this solution both satisfied his desire to be useful to other people and also enabled him to live up to his family responsibilities. Some men seem to feel that only other men are able to understand their vocational problems. But others, like this young executive, may be questioning their occupational identity so profoundly that a sensitive woman may be less threatening and more helpful in the long run than a male minister. A man, in other words, sometimes seems to need a surrogate mother to soothe his ruffled ego.

"I've held lots of sobbing men who were crying because of job problems," Polly Laughland, a fifty-year-old Unitarian pastor, said. "They need a sympathetic, caring listener more than anything else."

A young man may also find that he's into an unwise sexual relationship, but he feels too embarrassed to ask his parents to help straighten him out. His father, moreover, might be the authority figure in the family, and that discourages the boy from seeking out another man whom he would also expect to take a hard-line attitude toward his problem. It's quite logical for a young man in this situation to be drawn to a woman pastor.

One Presbyterian preacher, for example, found herself sitting across the desk from a young fellow who was wringing his hands and who seemed unable to find the right words to tell his story.

"Now come on, just tell me what it's all about," she coaxed.

"Don't tell my folks I'm here, okay?" he said. "They'd kill me if they knew."

"Don't worry about that. This is just between you and me. Now what's the matter?"

"Okay," he replied and took a deep breath. "For the last six months I've been going to a drive-in movie almost every night with this girl. We always park on the very back row, and we've had sexual intercourse every night. I don't want to marry her or anything. But now she's going out with somebody else, and I can't live without that sex. I've just got to have it."

As the boy looked down at the floor and lapsed into silence, the pastor realized what "nerve it must have taken for that kid to come in and tell me that. I'm still mid-Victorian when it comes to sexual things. I don't have any sympathy at all with premarital sex because I think God made intercourse for marriage. But I didn't dare look shocked or perturbed when he was talking or he might have stopped and run out of the room. I just kept a straight face and let him finish, even though I was churning inside."

When she was certain he had completed his story, the preacher said, "You know, even though you enjoyed it, that it isn't right, don't you?"

"Yes, I know that. That's why I haven't told my folks. They'd have a fit."

"I believe sex is a beautiful and wonderful thing when it's where God intended for it to be," the woman replied.

They had several meetings together, and the boy finally was able to resign himself to the loss of his lover. In reflecting on those counseling sessions, the pastor said, "I often wonder if he would have felt that he could approach a male minister and share something like that. Sex problems can be a very difficult topic to discuss with anyone, but it's especially hard if you expect your counselor to judge or criticize you. I think many people expect a woman to be less judgmental than a man."

But not every male parishioner is so eager to talk to a female pastor. When the preacher starts probing in sensitive areas, the man may try some rather ingenious techniques to discourage her by attempting to exploit suspected "feminine" weaknesses. One husband reluctantly agreed to go in and talk to a female minister about a marital problem he and his wife were having. The wife had told the pastor, whom we'll call Reverend Janice Jones, that her husband was drawing an adequate paycheck every week but was failing to turn enough money over to her to cover domestic expenses. Instead, he was spending the money at a local bar.

At the wife's urgent request, Janice asked the man into her study after church one Sunday morning and said, "Gee, I understand you and your wife are having a few little problems. I don't want to butt in where I'm not wanted, but if there's anything I can do to help, please let me know."

"We're not having any problems," he replied curtly.

"Well, I got the impression that your wife might be a little worried, and you're one of our favorite families here. I just want to let you know how much we think of you both. You know, I get a lot of people with problems who come through my office here—family finances, everything—and it might be that I could act as a sounding board."

"What did she tell you?" the man asked, glowering.

"Oh, she mentioned she doesn't feel she's getting quite enough to make ends meet at home, and—"

"That bastard! That bitch! Who the hell does she think she is, spreading stories like this around? She's always wasting my money . . ."

Instead of cowering at this outburst, Janice leaned forward and shot back a question: "Do you know what a bastard is?"

"What?" the man replied, taken somewhat aback.

"A bastard. Do you know what that word means?"

"Sure, uh, it's a kid, a person that's not legitimate—you know, a person who doesn't know who his parents are."

"That's right. Now did you mean to apply that word to your wife? Was she born illegitimately?"

"No, but . . ."

"No, she wasn't. Why did you say that about her, then?"

"Well . . ."

"Maybe you're saying and thinking a lot of things about her you don't really mean. Now I know both of you pretty well, and I don't know whether she has a real complaint or not. But I do know she's worried about you and your marriage, and I wish the two of you would come over here together later this afternoon. Let's talk together and see if we can't work something out."

By this time, the man had calmed down, and he agreed to come in later for some counseling. Soon, his marriage was back on a more even keel—but only because Janice had learned not to let a man buffalo her with profanity. "I don't have to go to the hairdresser to get my hair curled," she said. "It curls automatically when some of my parishioners start spewing forth obscenities in an effort to get me to quit probing into a particular problem they have. A burst of profanity is an indication that a person is really hurting, an indication I've really hit a sensitive point, a spot that's quite painful. The bad language is their way to defend themselves.

"But I always try to have a quick comeback ready to calm them down and let them know if that outburst was supposed to shock me because I'm a woman—forget it, brother! I try to use the same word they've used, but I put it in another context, such as getting them to define it. I'll just echo it right back, and that usually puts them off for a few seconds and allows me to take the offensive."

In this situation, the pastor wasn't worried that the man she was counseling might get physical or violent. But that thought may occasionally cross a pastor's mind when she's alone with a strapping male. A frantic wife asked Methodist pastor Norma Rust to talk to her husband because the husband, who had a jail record, frequently beat her. Norma, a small but courageous woman, agreed, and the man seemed eager at first to tell his side of the story in a logical, reasonable way. He wanted to convince the preacher that he, and not his wife, was right.

But as the interview progressed, the man stood up and started pacing around the room. "Sometimes he would crouch or squat in front of me, as though he was about to jump toward me," Norma recalled. "I began to wonder, 'What do I do if he *does* leap?' He kept pacing around behind me, and then when he walked around to face me, he'd look intently into my eyes, as though he was trying to stare me down."

On one occasion during the interview, the man stopped walking and said, "You're not afraid of me, are you?"

"No, should I be?" Norma replied. He seemed surprised at her steady, straightforward answer, and the counseling finished without any incident.

But even though she had remained calm outwardly, "I was doing a whale of a lot of thinking that he didn't know about," she admitted. "Down inside, my heart was pounding like crazy. He was definitely a very troubled young man, and his actions were a little anxiety-producing. I'm lucky my voice doesn't quaver when I'm afraid. I'm able to hide what's going on inside most of the time."

Occasionally, the physical advances may be sexual rather than violent. There has been a long tradition for male pastors to be regarded as idealized husbands or lovers in the eyes of their female parishioners. The woman parishioner's need to relate intimately to the male preacher may be satisfied through a deeply personal conversation or even innocent, casual physical contact, like a lingering handshake at the church door. On other occasions, the admiration of a woman for her pastor may turn into an actual seduction. The classic stereotype is the organist who runs off with her married preacher.

When a woman is in the pulpit, there is a reverse sexual syndrome that seems to operate in some parishes. Counseling sessions between the female minister and a male parishioner are the most likely situations to produce these amorous overtures. "When you're dealing with religious and spiritual things, you get into the emotions," Methodist Joanne Whitcomb observes. "You can see how all kinds of things could happen in a counseling situation. There are some men I do not want to see alone at my parsonage for any reason. And when I'm counseling a man, I'd never sit on the same couch, unless he happened to be a close personal friend."

Like Joanne, some other female pastors have also managed to avoid the problem of passes from male parishioners by remaining physically aloof. Baptist Ruth Thompson, a handsome, silver-haired woman, says flatly, "I don't have any problems. I grew up in a time when there was none of this touching business. I was told male ministers never put their hands on girls or women. And girls going into Christian work weren't careless in their contacts with fellows. Since I'm a rather formal person, that was an easy tradition for me to follow. But I've learned in the last few years there is a warmth that's communicated by touching. I find it means something to hold a hand during a prayer in the hospital. But I have very strong feelings about ministers who have sexual problems with parishioners. I can only say that somewhere along the line they've been too careless and opened themselves up."

Fifty-year-old Polly Laughland says that "for a long time I didn't touch anyone for any reason. But a lot of us have been trying to break through this touching business. I'm apt to express concern or caring for someone by taking an arm or hand. I have had this misinterpreted by one wife: other parishioners have told me this woman thought, 'She's trying to run off with my husband!' Of course, I had no such intention."

The Unitarians, Polly says, are "a very kissy denomination. In a big group, there's a lot of strenuous hugging. At our church last month one man said, 'I like having a woman minister. She gives good sermons, she's nice to look at, and I can kiss her after the service.' "

Things have gotten out of hand a few times, however. Polly had a man with career problems come to her for counseling, and she found he had a real need "to reaffirm his masculine identity. I moved to say goodbye, to wish him well, and he gave me a thank-you-for-helping-me sort of hug." But the hug got a little harder and more passionate than she felt was appropriate, so she gave him a "gentle push" away and with a laugh said, "Not here, not now."

Despite the possibility of unwanted sexual advances, Polly feels that the "touching tendency is a good thing. People need to get closer to each other, get in touch with their emotions and feelings. Women on the whole haven't been all that good about it. Many are too standoffish. I worked one summer as a chaplain in a state hospital with senile females. Many were not even coherent, and the only way you could reach them was to touch. A lot of relating there is done by touching, stroking, rocking. I think it's a valid way of ministry."

But sometimes men don't come in for valid counseling reasons at all. Their primary intention is to seduce the woman pastor, and that problem requires a firm hand—sometimes a firm physical hand. Margaret Frerichs, who is now in her fifties, has dealt with enough men in enough parishes that she can almost anticipate those who are likely to become amorous: "I have an inkling beforehand that a guy might make a pass at me in the way he holds on a little too long when he shakes hands at the church door. And there is usually a certain look in the eyes."

She has also had some problems when she lives alone in a parsonage and has her study there. "Anybody can drop in and see me, and I've had to deal pretty firmly with a couple of married men who got amorous," she said. "They came in under the pretext of counseling, or making an official visit, and they were reasonable enough men, not maniacs." But action was necessary in each case. As one man tried to grab her, she gave him a shove and said, "This can't be. I appreciate your feelings, but you know this can't be."

"The situation is manageable as long as you don't run into somebody who is mentally unstable," she noted in recounting this incident.

Druecillar Fordham has also counseled men alone at her Baptist church, and on occasion they have indicated from the outset of the conversation that they had other things in mind than advice. One man phoned her and said he had a spiritual problem to talk over. But when he arrived at her office, he devoted only a few seconds to the spiritual problem and then launched into an appraisal of Druecillar: "You know, you're nice-looking. Why do you want to settle down with this sort of thing? Let me tell you what I can do for you . . ."

"Hold on," she interrupted in a businesslike tone of voice. "I thought you came for specific counseling, but now you're talking about something else."

Even if her commanding voice isn't enough to stop them, she says she's never had to use physical force with any of her ardent admirers. "I have a look that will put them off me," she notes with a twinkle in her eye.

Because of the pastor's need to counsel men as well as women, unmarried female preachers run into the problem of gossip even if there is no justification for it. Norma Rust says that when townsfolk see a man come to her house three or four times, she will inevitably hear from a parishioner, "Hey, Norma, I hear you're going with So-and-So."

Norma, with tongue in cheek, replies, "Hey, you're way behind the times. Let me tell you about the latest one . . ."

"They have had me going with so many fellows it's ridiculous," she said, shaking her head. "Sometimes it's just a little provoking. I think, 'For goodness' sake, don't they have anything else to do?' To nip any gossip in the bud, I'll tell the pastor-parish relations committee, 'In case you hear or have heard I'm dating So-and-So, I want you to know that I'm not. And in case you doubt me, I invite you to call him.' Of course, I don't feel I'm supposed to explain why each person comes to my door. I'm answerable to my church leaders, but not to the point of betraying confidences."

Difficulties in counseling individual male parishioners can require bluntness or toughness by a woman minister. But a more finely tuned pastoral virtuosity may be necessary when both a man and a woman walk arm in arm into the church office for advice. Take the case of a young unmarried couple who are running into difficulties because they're living together. One savvy young female preacher has pointed out to such couples that their problems may stem from the fact that they haven't made enough of a commitment to one another. "In marriage, there's the idea of a covenant, which involves a special kind of commitment," she explained. "Tensions develop with a couple who are living together because often one person wants more of a commitment than the other does. I'm not saying the people living together are necessarily always wrong, but I do think the institution of marriage is a good thing.

"My husband and I lived together in communal situations before we were married," she says frankly, "and I know the difference in the nature of the commitment. I sometimes share my own experience with the people I counsel, so they know I know what I'm talking about. Here's the approach I might take: In marriage, when you get angry at your husband, you can't just say, 'Well, I won't have to be angry tomorrow because I won't be with him.' Marriage brings out deeper things in a person than living together does. People who only live together will often reject my statement that marriage is important, but I know what I'm saying is true."

When a man and woman have decided to get married, a female minister may take a different approach to counseling than her male counterpart. This contrast in styles is exemplified by Jim and Susan Gertmenian, the co-pastors of two Presbyterian churches in New York's Catskill Mountains.

"I concentrate more on pragmatic issues, such as how the couple are going to divide their use of the car, while Susan is more sensitive to their underlying feelings and emotions," Jim explained.

"I've learned a lot from my own therapy and my own Gestalt exercises," Susan said. "If I see someone tightening up, I'll point that out and ask if the tightness is indicative of any kind of inner feeling. When one person speaks the whole time for the other person, I usually point this out. I'll say, 'Look what's happening here! So-and-So is doing all the talking. Is there something you would like to say that differs from what he is saying? How do you feel about having him speak for you all the time?' "

On one occasion, Susan protested that a silent bride-to-be was getting red in the face while her fiancé was doing all the talking. The young woman replied, "Oh, I agree with everything he's said."

"They wanted everything to go smoothly, but now that they've gotten married, that's turned out to be a problem," Susan said. "He's an obsessive talker. Even though she has a lot of things to say, she doesn't have a chance."

Jim believes that the reluctance of such couples to express their true feelings stems from a desire "to put up a façade for the minister who's going to marry them. They don't want us to think there's anything wrong. I'm sure they have some fear that if they get into an argument, we'll say, 'Well, we're not going to marry you.' That's not true, of course, but it still bothers them."

Occasionally, though, ministers have encountered couples with such monumental problems that even the most skillful premarital counseling is doomed to failure. The pastor's desire to reconcile these wounds is sometimes so strong that she may still forge ahead and try to close impossible breaches in the relationship.

Doris, a rural Southern minister, was confronted with a number of shotgun marriages in her church. In a typical counseling session, some glowering parents marched their young daughter and her sullen boy friend into Doris's office and said, "Marry them!"

"Do they want to get married?" the pastor asked.

"She's pregnant and they have to get married," the father replied.

"Well, let's discuss the marriage vows," Doris said, looking toward the young people. "Do you expect to stay married until death do you part?"

"No," the boy said. "We don't want it to last. We have to marry because we have to give this baby a name."

At that, the girl started crying. It was evident that she loved the boy more than he loved her.

"Well, you know abortion is a possibility," Doris said gently. "And sometimes we can find a family that will raise the baby if you don't want an abortion and don't want to get married either." Doris had succeeded on one occasion in getting a couple in this same situation to agree to an adoption, but she knew there wasn't much of a chance of that in this case.

"No, we want to go ahead with the wedding," the father said.

"And then what, after you get married?" Doris asked.

"We'll probably separate after the baby gets its name," the boy answered.

The pastor tried to counsel and reason with the kids and the parents, but she realized her efforts were hopeless. Still, she decided to go ahead with the wedding. "I felt reluctance about performing such a marriage, and I know some ministers wouldn't have done it," she said later. "But I always felt they would get married anyway—just go to a justice of the peace. I had the hope that the religious ceremony and whatever counseling I could do would help some, and in a few cases it did. But it was certainly depressing. I often married them and just hoped for the best."

This flexible attitude toward marriage counseling also characterizes the approach many female pastors take toward one of their potentially most depressing church responsibilities—the funeral. Baptist pastor Ruth Thompson says, "I love to put a good funeral together. There are some male pastors who won't bury anybody except those who have been baptized. My feeling is that everybody has been created in the image of God, and it seems to me they should be buried with some dignity."

Even though Ruth is willing to reach out and, in a profoundly maternal sense, gather the unchurched into her funeral ceremonies, she does put certain limits on her involvement: "I don't say anything I can't say with a clear conscience. You can always safely say, 'They are in God's hands, where we all will be one day.' Then you can use Scripture and let it fall where it may."

One of the main reasons that Ruth refuses to stand on tradition in conducting funeral services for non-Christians is that "it can be a witness to the survivors that you're willing to conduct the funeral and be gracious to them. There's no reason to scold them or reject them. They always feel guilty. They tell me, 'It was good of you to come because we haven't been to church for years.' I may say to them, 'Remember that the Lord knows when you're suffering, and he cares.' Sometimes, if they're bitter, they'll say, 'Oh, I don't believe that.' But other times they'll say, 'Yes, I know, but I don't deserve God's care because I haven't been very faithful.'

"People are very open and tender at those times. You can say a lot of things at a time of sorrow that you can't say at other times. I imagine I'll always be willing to conduct funerals for both church and non-church people and be gracious toward them."

When a parishioner who is committed to the faith dies, the pastor's own conviction and her compassion and empathy for the survivors can help turn a funeral into an occasion of joy. Linda Harter was in charge of her Presbyterian parish one week while her co-pastor husband, Bill, was away at a church conference. A very influential member of their church was rushed to the hospital with a heart attack during that period, and Linda got a call at 7 A.M. to join the family at his bedside.

"I have an army of baby sitters, but many had been partying all weekend and I wasn't sure I could get anybody to stay with my four children," Linda said. "But I found one who could help and in fifteen minutes she was running up the street toward our house."

When Linda reached the hospital, she immediately sought out the wife of the sick man and had a short prayer with her. Soon afterward, the doctor walked into the waiting room and said, "I'm sorry, but he's gone." The wife began crying at the shock of this announcement and the sense of separation she felt. Linda gave a brief prayer: "Thank you, God, that he's with you. Help us."

Soon, after the initial shock had worn off, a sense of affirmation, and finally of joy, crept into the family's attitude toward the death. And Linda's own beliefs helped reinforce this positive attitude. "They had a real sense that the man was with God; they really believed," Linda said. "This man was a committed Christian, and the source of their joy was that he was a believer. Because he was a good friend, I myself had a physical reaction to his death at the pit of my stomach. But I accept death as another milestone in life, a doorway to eternal life with God. Death is inevitable, but if God has prepared the way for us, there's nothing to be afraid of."

Linda remembered that a feeling of peace took over at the hospital, "and then the joy came through as we went back to the family's home and contacted other family members and friends. This family's attitude was a great witness to the community: they showed an awareness of the real meaning of death and a profound acceptance of the resurrection."

Perhaps the ultimate in caring for a person at the time of death was demonstrated by Unitarian pastor Polly Laughland. An undertaker called her and asked if she would say a few words for a penniless woman who had died without any family or friends. The undertaker planned to cremate the body, but he felt it was somehow wrong to throw the deceased into the oven without a short ceremony.

"It was just me and the plywood box," Polly said. "I put my robe on and read the Twenty-third Psalm and a few more words. No one else was there, not even the undertaker. It was kind of a weirdie, but I wouldn't have done it if I had thought it was stupid. This poor woman deserved some little acknowledgment of the fact that she had lived. It was a touching thing."

In addition to these conventional ways of loving, caring and reconciling in their congregations, some women pastors also bring special skills to their pastoral work because they have been trained in certain professions that are dominated by women. Take the nursing profession, for example. Although there are a few male nurses, the overwhelming majority in this field are females. Jean Arthur became a registered nurse before she was ordained. She has found that her medical skills have been invaluable in ministering to her congregations.

Jean takes the blood pressure of ailing members of her parish and gives them preliminary medical checkups as part of her regular visitation program. "I think both spiritual and physical healing are very important," she explained. "I can't stand preaching to sick people. I first want to know what's wrong physically, what I can do to help."

Her concern for both the physical and spiritual well-being of her parishioners has on at least one occasion helped to save a person's life. One man was in the hospital with a serious kidney problem, and he was attached to a dialysis machine. "That machine and prayer were the only things that were keeping him alive," Jean recalled.

But the doctors had been giving him so many antibiotics that he was turning into a "penicillin factory," Jean explained. "He had started making his own penicillin—the antibiotic was actually growing in his body. I had had experience with this problem as a missionary in India, but the attending physician didn't know anything about it."

The man's pulse and blood pressure declined to a dangerously low level, and the doctor finally gave up on him. When Jean tried to convince the physician about her "penicillin factory" observation, he replied, "That's impossible!" and he refused to do anything about it.

Finally, Jean took a bowl containing the patient's vomit, which reeked with the smell of penicillin, and placed it under the doctor's nose.

The physician exclaimed, "Did this come out of that guy?"

"Yes," Jean replied wearily. "That's what I've been trying to tell you."

The doctor immediately ordered fluids to clear the antibiotic out of the patient's system, and the young man soon recovered. "He's home working on a full-time basis, and he's become more active in the church too," Jean said with a knowing smile. "I'm not saying every minister should take up medicine, but it's certainly a good thing to know for a pastor who visits sick people."

Jean Arthur might be regarded as a pastoral specialist in that she has medical skills that make her especially valuable when she's dealing with parishioners who are in poor health. In a sense, all of the counseling and personal relations work, which women ministers seem to do so well, is a pastoral specialty that has been recognized as such by several institutions in our society—the military service, hospitals and universities. These institutions have hired "spiritual specialists," or chaplains, to concentrate primarily on counseling. Although men have dominated these jobs in the past, the chaplaincies seem a likely candidate to become one of the strongest power bases of ordained women.

CHAPTER SEVEN

The Spiritual Specialists

The small boy lay serenely on his bed. He had an almost cherubic expression on his smooth, pale face, and Air Force chaplain Lorraine Potter found herself thinking for a moment that he looked normal, like any other sleeping six-year-old child. But then the stark reality of the situation flooded into her consciousness again, and that churning, acidic feeling at the pit of her stomach returned. The boy, she knew, was not well at all. He had been smashed by an automobile while he was riding his bicycle, and he lay now in a coma, hanging between life and death. Although no gashes or bruises were visible as he lay on his back, with the covers pulled up to his small chest, he had received a terrible blow to the back of his head and was suffering from severe brain damage.

"Oh, please, Captain Potter, help us pray," cried the boy's mother, whose husband was stationed on the military base.

Lorraine turned away from the bed and looked at the distraught, tear-streaked faces of the parents. "What do you think we should pray for?" she asked quietly.

"Oh, for him to live, for my son to live," the mother said. Then she shook her head and began to sob again. "But if he does live, there'll be permanent brain damage, won't there? Oh, I just don't know what to pray for."

The churning feeling in Lorraine's stomach grew more insistent, and she looked back at the boy. Confusing, heart-rending thoughts kept racing through her mind: "This little kid hasn't even lived—he's only six . . . and those poor people who hit him, what must they feel now? . . . but I'm not sure what to pray for . . . I want him to get well, yet I don't want his parents to hold on too strongly because he probably won't be like he was before if he does live."

Lorraine finally cleared her throat, tightened her nauseous stomach and began to lead the parents through a prayer: "O God, we want him to live, but we don't know what that will mean, what his life is going to be. Help us to pray." The parents then opened up and expressed their own feelings, but none of them knew exactly what they wanted, what would be the best result in this tragic situation. Lorraine was relieved when she finally left to get the mother and father some coffee. She felt very "mechanical," running errands for them, but that seemed the most helpful thing she could do under the circumstances.

When the petite, blue-eyed captain arrived back at her apartment that night, she laid aside her blue Air Force uniform, stretched out on her bed and tried to forget her chaplaincy duties that day. But she couldn't get that hospital scene out of her mind. The thoughts of the outwardly serene but doomed child lying in that hospital bed continued to plague her. She couldn't sleep, and the nausea became more intense. Finally, Lorraine rushed into her bathroom and fumbled for the light. Pulling her short, curly brown hair back from her face, she leaned over the toilet and vomited.

The boy lived for about a week and a half after Lorraine started working on his case. He had started to come out of the coma at one point, but it was evident that if he had lived, at least one side of his body would have been completely paralyzed. Lorraine had to believe that God's will had been done.

As a military chaplain in the Air Force's huge Wilford Hall Medical Center in San Antonio, Texas, Lorraine, an ordained American Baptist minister, constantly encounters difficult situations that tax her counseling and pastoral skills to the limit. But she thrives on crises. Helping others to deal with overwhelming emotional and spiritual challenges is her primary interest as a pastor, and there's no better place to wrestle with profound human problems than a chaplaincy.

"People are asking more faith questions here than any other place," she explained. "They may not talk about 'God,' but that's what they're dealing with. And in those situations, people are willing to open themselves up to receive help from whoever is near them. I try to help humans in crisis get in touch with their own Christian faith, but I don't impart a doctrine or emphasize my own convictions."

Lorraine has forced herself to confront even the most distasteful heartbreaking situations so that she can become a more effective minister. "The hardest thing for me personally is working with seriously ill children," she confessed. "I think they've been cheated out of life. But I've intentionally chosen to work with them and their parents, and it's gotten easier."

As a military chaplain, Lorraine does everything that her male counterparts are required to do. She preaches to servicemen and their dependents on her base, stands the base chaplaincy duty for a twenty-four-hour period once a week and has regular office hours to counsel those in need. She could be transferred to any Air Force base that needs a chaplain, including bases in a combat zone. The Navy and Army have female chaplains whose duties are similar to Lorraine's.

Outside the military, a growing number of civilian female hospital chaplains are also dealing with patients who have serious physical problems. Other chaplains are concentrating on crises of the mind— identity crises that are wracking students on the nation's university campuses. But whether these pastors choose the military, the hospital or the university chaplaincy, they must all be regarded as spiritual specialists. Most parish ministers are generalists in that they spread their time and efforts fairly equally between preaching, church administration and counseling, but the chaplains are relieved of many of the church-building and fund-raising headaches. Although they may do some preaching in an institution's chapel or organize special events, their main purpose is to provide spiritual advice and nurturance to those in the institution.

The campus chaplain's job is to help guide the student in his search for identity and introduce him to the spiritual and moral dimensions of his existence. College students are in school to acquire knowledge and prepare themselves for the working world. But they are also constantly exploring who they are, what they believe, why they should choose one life-style over another. One technique the female campus specialists use is to assume the role of substitute mother and apply firm but loving moral pressure on young people who are looking for someone to tell them what's right and what's wrong.

Abigail Evans, chaplain at Columbia University and associate pastor at Manhattan's Broadway Presbyterian Church, believes in using this forthright approach with students. "I don't believe in being wishy-washy," says Abigail, who is the mother of four boys. "One of the biggest problems for young people is that they don't really know where the church or individual ministers stand on moral issues."

When she's counseling a boy and girl who have been living together before they get married, for example, Abigail is very frank about stating her views on premarital sex. "I tell them that I feel sad, in a way," she says. "I tell them there's a certain loss that occurs when you give yourself to a person in that way. I've seen many girls who have given themselves to so many fellows that they have nothing left to give. They have lost the sense of having a fellow look at them as a total human being. These girls become objects in their own eyes."

Abigail speaks from her experience not only as a college chaplain but also as a former missionary in Brazil. She got to know many of the prostitutes who lived in the "zona," or red-light district; often they would drop by her house to talk. "They had that same sense of loss," Abigail says. "They knew they could never get married and have children because no man would have them. Men would feel they had given everything away. It's not just a physical thing—it's also emotional," she added.

Abigail sees many female students who are still virgins and are confused about how to respond to their boy friends who visit from out of town. When girls pose this question to her, the chaplain asks them plainly, "What do you want to have left to give when you find a person you want to spend the rest of your life with? There's a certain investment in an intimate sexual relationship. You give a part of yourself that you can't regain."

Although Abigail's firm, maternal approach may be appropriate for younger students, a peer-to-peer counseling session can be more helpful for those who are older or more mature. When a female student's problems involve serious marital and career crises, a woman chaplain is usually better equipped by her own life experiences to deal with the issues than a man.

"The biggest problem of my older women students is a low sense of their personal identity," says a chaplain at a West Coast university. She cites the case of a married female graduate student who came for counseling because she was having an affair with another man and felt guilty about it. "What it boiled down to is that she had married a very capable career man who was devoted primarily to his work and only secondarily to his wife," the minister explained. "The young wife felt left out. Then she met someone else who made her feel her worth as a woman and who gave her personal, sexual and intellectual stimulation. But she felt terribly guilty about it because she really loved her husband."

The chaplain, who had wrestled with the question of her own female identity, tried to help the student understand how she got herself into such a fix. "She was very attractive and was used to having a lot of attention," the pastor explained. "But after she got tied down to a husband, she found he wasn't paying any attention to her."

The young woman interpreted his preoccupation with his career as rejection of her, so she started finding faults with herself. She seemed obsessed with listing her own inadequacies: "I guess I'm not a very good sexual partner . . . I know I can't cook that well . . . as for intelligence, well, my grades aren't the greatest . . ."

The chaplain, by sharing some of her own identity struggles, was able to show the student that her problems were rooted in her own low estimate of herself, rather than in her husband's career concerns. The student gradually started to rebuild her life. She developed a different attitude toward her studies and gained enough confidence to start thinking seriously about a career. She also ended the affair with the other man.

Another growing problem that college chaplains are confronting is homosexuality, and female ministers have been forced to take positions on that difficult issue just as their male counterparts have. There is pressure on chaplains who affirm traditional standards of morality to bend their values to conform to the position of militant campus gay groups. Some traditionalists, like the Reverend Abigail Evans, refuse to budge, however. Abigail even shared a campus office at Columbia with representatives of the gay liberation movement, but she remained unequivocally opposed to their objectives.

"My understanding of the Christian position is that homosexuality is not how God intended for us to be," she says flatly.

When a gay student comes to her for help with a conflict over sexual identity, Abigail tries to find out why the person is a homosexual and whether or not he's just experimenting with his sexuality. "A lot of times I find that the supposedly gay students aren't even sure they *are* homosexuals," she says. "But now that it's free and open at Columbia, they decide they are latent homosexuals." She has also found that, as a result of the new sexual openness, "people who may not be homosexuals become homosexuals."

But Abigail does not try to counsel with homosexuals on a long-term basis. "I try to get them to see a psychiatric counselor," she says.

Connie Parvey, a Lutheran chaplain at Harvard and the Massachusetts Institute of Technology, is somewhat more equivocal with students who express homosexual preferences. "I feel that we're in a very different position today than was the New Testament church," she says. "In the situation Paul faced in Corinth, there was a great deal of licentiousness and impure living. But most of the people I see who are homosexual or lesbian are just struggling human beings trying to live a decent life and have some experience of love, warmth and affection. Most of the people I counsel are not what you'd call really immoral people. They've had a tough time of it. So I try to start with them where they are, and help them understand why they're doing it."

As for the morality of homosexuality, Connie says, "I don't say it's right, and I don't say it's wrong. There are always moral and ethical questions in any relationship. The most important moral question is, 'Who is my neighbor and how am I treating him?' "

Because female chaplains are still a relatively unusual phenomenon, they sometimes find it helps to wear some outward mark of their official position, such as a clerical collar. Connie, a tall, slim honey-blond in her early forties, got a call during her first week as a Harvard chaplain to hurry to a Boston hospital. A married female student, who had been in a serious automobile wreck, was lying in a coma, and her grief-stricken mother needed spiritual and emotional support. The girl's husband had been killed when their car ran head on into a truck, and her mother wanted a minister to be present in case the girl regained consciousness.

"I knew I just couldn't appear on the scene there as another woman," said Connie. "I'd be taken as a good friend or a social worker or some stranger helping out, and what would it mean to the student to open her eyes and see me there?"

She had never worn a collar before because she was very "anti-clerical," but a friend in California had sent her a high-camp collar with the word "Connie" embroidered in bright pink across the front. She hurriedly took a razor blade, cut off the embroidery, pinned the collar on and hung a large cross around her neck. "I was clearly identified," she recalls. "I felt so odd wearing this collar thing and was hoping nobody would see me. But as soon as I got into the institutional context of the hospital, it was just magic."

She walked up hesitantly to the receptionist at the hospital and said, "I'm Pastor Parvey from Harvard."

There was a flash of surprise on the nurse's face as she looked Connie up and down, but she quickly recovered and replied, "Oh, we've been waiting for you."

Connie was then ushered in to see the mother and doctors, who explained the background of the case. "I wouldn't have been able to make the progress with the doctors that I did if I had not been wearing that clerical collar," Connie said. "They immediately recognized me as a fellow professional, and I got in to the intensive care unit to see the young woman, which is what the mother wanted. She was concerned that her daughter might die in an unfaithful state."

A week later, as the girl began to come out of her coma, Connie, now generally recognized as the pastor on the case, was able to employ her counseling skills as a specialist at reconciliation. She acted as an intermediary between the girl's mother and the doctors over the question of whether or not to tell the female student about her husband's death.

"The girl needed a second operation," said Connie, "and the doctors had instructed the staff not to tell her that her husband had died. But she was calling for him even though she was only conscious once in a while. It was getting confusing for her because her mother was coming in to visit, but her husband wasn't. The girl's mother was put in the position of having to make up stories about why the husband wasn't appearing on the scene. It put her in a very difficult position of credibility with her daughter."

After much discussion with the mother and the doctors, Connie was able to help the doctors understand the "human side" of the situation. "They could see that they were putting the mother in a compromising position by delaying telling the girl," the pastor explained. The doctors finally relented, and the mother broke the news to her daughter. Connie came in later to add her support.

"It's true," she told the young woman softly. "We've been very concerned about it and we've talked about it a lot. Your mother has been in a very difficult position because she wanted you to know and she felt compromised by not being able to tell you." As soon as the girl knew the truth, she was grief-stricken, but she soon began to recover more quickly.

In retrospect, Connie believes there were elements in her counseling approach—especially in her dealings with the student's mother—which were distinctively female. Although Connie aggressively used her chaplain's authority to take the initiative with the doctors, she was careful not to take command of the situation, as the mother had expected a male pastor might do, and tell the mother what to do. Instead, "I showed her alternatives and gave her psychological support," the pastor said. "I wouldn't let her lean on me."

At first, Connie was worried that "I couldn't function as a pastor for her because what she needed was a man. She was used to having a man around in a crisis situation—either her husband, who had died recently, or her male pastor at home." But the chaplain discovered that by working with her and helping her make her own decisions, the woman gained strength in her new independence.

"You know," she told Connie afterward, "you acted like a pastor, but also like a friend. You gave me so much confidence to handle the situation."

"Part of the woman's reaction," Connie noted, "is that she saw me as a woman functioning competently in my role, and it helped her function more competently as a woman in her role."

Although Connie Parvey is primarily a campus chaplain, her work in this case spilled over into the role of hospital chaplain and shows how interchangeable the specialized counseling skills of all the chaplains can be. But similar as the jobs are in some respects, there are also many differences. While the campus chaplain's duties usually focus on young people with emotional and spiritual crises, hospital chaplains often find themselves dealing with older patients, many of whom are facing serious debilitating illnesses, or even death. Female hospital chaplains have found that they are especially well suited to counsel women who confront these serious and often intimate crises of health.

Reverend Jean Gilbert, a chaplain at New York Hospital and at Memorial Sloan-Kettering in New York City, says, "I think the chaplain has an opportunity to deal with people on levels no other staff people can. Even the social workers get caught up in administrative things, but they're part of the institution, and I'm not. I'm sort of an ombudsman. Patient advocacy is important to me."

In her work at Memorial Sloan-Kettering, one of the nation's leading cancer centers, she often has to counsel women with breast cancer. The very fact that she is a woman encourages other women to talk with her, and she tries to make things even easier by her style of dress. She avoids a white hospital coat and wears street clothes, usually pants and shirts, to help make herself more approachable. "Talking about things like a mastectomy is easy for me," she says. "I know that it's hard for some male pastors. They're apprehensive about talking about a woman's body."

Jean, a diminutive, quiet young woman with a quick smile, usually starts a conversation with a mastectomy patient by asking, "Tell me how it's going for you—what's it like?" Many women will express the hope that it's their last cancer, that the doctors will catch it all in this operation, but Jean knows that many fears lurk behind this hope. "They're afraid they might die or be disfigured," she explained. "I find it helps to lay these fears out on the table. Then people become less afraid."

After the operation, women go through a process of grieving over the loss of their breast. "Many women think they shouldn't feel that this loss is a painful experience," says Jean. "Our culture has done a number on us in terms of our not being open about expressing fear and pain."

Although traditionally the presence of the chaplain is somehow supposed to facilitate the presence of God in crisis situations, Jean does not push her patients into prayer. "I pray with patients who ask it and when it's a meaningful experience," she says. "But it's very rare for me to do that. When I do pray, I might say that life is often difficult for us to understand and makes no sense to us, and that it's hard to be faithful when the world seems to be falling apart. Then I pray for the presence of God."

In these critical moments, even when death is imminent, Jean says, "I don't feel any need to evangelize, but I do feel a need to witness." Witnessing, for Jean, can mean confronting a person with the truth she may not want to hear. The chaplain talked on a number of occasions with a woman who was suffering from cancer but refused to acknowledge she was dying. She left the hospital still denying the seriousness of her illness, and her husband reinforced the notion that she was not very ill.

"You're going to be okay," he'd tell her.

Although the woman was a religious person, she clung to the idea that having faith would cure her, and that somehow her illness was tied in with her lack of faith. "She gave me an example of someone who had lived long with cancer because of a strong belief in God," Jean said.

Jean told the woman, "Don't feel that you're sick because you're not faithful. Faithful people *do* die. They don't always get well."

"It's hard to confront attitudes like that directly," says Jean. "But to let them go on is not dealing with the truth."

Elements of both the campus and hospital chaplaincies may also be found in the military chaplaincy, but an even more distinctively masculine aura, which is not as characteristic of the other institutions, pervades the military service. The military is a man's world, with physical requirements, rigid command structures and tough-talking, rough-and-tumble traditions. Why would Lorraine Potter, a tiny, twenty-eight-year-old Air Force captain, get involved in such a masculine field?

"I grew up with an image of a woman in the pulpit because my mother is a lay Baptist minister," Lorraine explained. "The ministry was always an option for me because I heard her give sermons as a supply, or substitute, preacher and knew she had been a regular church pastor before I was born. So it was a possible thing for me. It wasn't until I got to seminary that I realized people were asking questions like, 'Why does a woman want to go into the ordained ministry?'"

Lorraine underwent a profound crisis of faith as she entered seminary because "my father had just died and my concept of God wasn't helping me deal with that situation. But I gradually reached some conclusions: I believe that if we commit ourselves, somehow God will help us through difficult situations and show us something about our fellow human beings and how God works in our lives. God took the worst human experience—the cruelty of other men denying and crucifying Christ—and transformed that into something which, for those who believe, is the most exciting and beautiful event of history. If God did it then, he can do it now, with other situations that seem very painful."

Lorraine found during a practical seminary training program in a state mental hospital that as a chaplain she "had an opportunity to relate to people where they were hurting." The hospital chaplaincy, a pastoral specialty that stressed the counseling function during times of crisis, was a "tool or an enabler," the captain said.

Having decided to embark on a career as a chaplain, Lorraine learned in her post-seminary training as a hospital chaplain in New Haven, Connecticut, that she had a knack for counseling men—even those with intimate problems of sexual identity. After she had progressed in the hospital chaplaincy program, she was assigned to supervise some new trainee chaplains. One of her charges was a young male chaplain who had been propositioned by a homosexual patient he was counseling. He was concerned about whether or not he could continue to work with the homosexual client.

"This young minister was uncertain what was happening inside himself," said Lorraine. "He didn't have the issue of homosexuality under control and the proposition raised a lot of questions for him personally."

After discussing his feelings openly with Lorraine, he was able to get in touch with his own sexual feelings and could counsel successfully with his patient. "I could never have discussed this with a male supervisor," he told Lorraine candidly. "I would have felt very threatened to admit to another man that I had been propositioned by a homosexual. I'm grateful we can talk about this."

After such successful counseling experiences with men, it was natural for Lorraine to consider the military chaplaincy among her job options after she completed her training as a hospital specialist. The Air Force offered a good three-year program that provided considerable practical experience, and the heavily masculine flavor of the military gave her no particular feelings of apprehension. She had learned that she could handle most counseling situations as well as any man, and she knew she had the edge on her male colleagues in some respects.

After Lorraine donned her blue Air Force uniform and pinned on her silver captain's bars and chaplain's cross, she soon discovered that her military milieu presented her with challenges that were different from an ordinary hospital ministry. For one thing, a steady parade of young men who were in search of the meaning of life—specifically, the meaning of *military* life—trooped in and out of her office. Their feelings toward talking with her may be summed up by the comments of one eighteen-year-old who wanted to get out of the Air Force.

"I'm glad I'm talking to a woman," he told Lorraine.

"Why is that?" she replied. "Am I so different?"

"Yes. I'm not sure I could tell a man I couldn't hack it."

Although Lorraine looks younger than she is, she says that these young servicemen "see I'm a little older than they are when they notice the captain's bars. They assume I've been around for a while and can get them out of what they don't like, or help them into what they do like."

But Lorraine has experienced some rough weather in the Air Force precisely because of the fact that she is a woman. She had been counseling one young man about some sex problems, and after one session, he turned to her as they were waiting for an elevator and said, "By the way, chaplain, what are you doing Saturday night?"

Lorraine didn't hesitate to set him straight. "That is an inappropriate comment," she said. "If you want a direct answer, I'm not doing anything Saturday night, but I don't need an excuse to turn you down."

She felt this stern, unequivocal retort was necessary because "this young man had serious problems in his relationships with women. He wanted to manipulate them by getting them into a sexual relationship. That's what he was trying to do to me. He probably thought if I got personally interested in him, I'd give him help I wouldn't give otherwise."

Male chaplains sometimes present similar problems. A fellow chaplain came to her to discuss one of his patients, but it became evident that he had more personal concerns on his mind.

"He asked me to counsel with him, but he stipulated that we do it secretly and not discuss it with other chaplains," said Lorraine. "I got very uncomfortable because I didn't know him very well, and I felt that through his secrecy he wanted to establish a relationship with me because I was female."

Lorraine thought fast and suggested a team counseling setup, where she and another chaplain could meet with this man regularly.

"I'm getting vibrations from you which make this necessary," she told him frankly. "And besides, I couldn't counsel anyone if I couldn't discuss the problem with other professionals," she added.

The chaplain accepted her conditions and helped her choose a co-counselor. "He was having marriage problems, and if he had had only a female counselor it could have been very easy for him to relate to me as a kind of surrogate wife," explained Lorraine.

Although Captain Lorraine Potter has found that most of her fellow chaplains feel positive about her presence, she has run into a few who resent her and are worried that she may endanger their own authority. One older male chaplain, who was known for his liberal use of profanity, told her bluntly, "I don't think a woman should be a chaplain."

"Why do you feel that way?" she asked.

Ignoring her question, he continued, "I'm not going to change how I talk just because you're here. You just do your work and leave my territory alone."

"I'm not expecting anyone to give me support," Lorraine replied. "As long as I'm allowed to do what I'm capable of doing, I'm all right. I can't minister to everyone, and I don't feel everyone has to accept me here, either. This hospital is big enough for you and me and quite a few others."

Lorraine admits she doesn't have "much authority" in the service. But she knows she's a competent professional and is confident that the top-level officers in the chaplaincy will recognize that and not be swayed in their judgment of her by occasional anti-female criticism. Although it would be easy for a small, friendly young woman to become cowed by the dominant presence of so many men, Lorraine and other successful female chaplains seem to realize that as women they have some unique qualities to bring to their jobs.

As Lutheran campus chaplain Connie Parvey puts it, "My presence brings out people's feminine side more. Some of the students tell me that I communicate a feeling of warmth, compassion, and a sense that it's okay to care." One male student told Connie, "You've opened up to me a sense of my sensitive side, and reawakened my social awareness. I had gotten so into myself and into my professional work that I lost touch with the world around me."

"Somehow men don't convey these feelings to each other," says Connie. "They convey more a sense of ordering, reasoning and thinking things through with dispassion. The woman's image definitely does convey a different message."

As female ministers open up the male-dominated chaplaincies, another masculine religious stronghold—the rabbinate of liberal Judaism—has been breached by ordained women. "It should never happen," traditional Jews may say, but it is happening, as Jewish seminaries are beginning to turn out increasing numbers of female rabbis.

CHAPTER EIGHT

A Foot
in the Synagogue Door

When Rabbi Sandy Sasso stood up to speak, she knew she was in a tenuous position. Her listeners were members of a Conservative Jewish congregation—a branch of Judaism which does not yet ordain female rabbis. Sandy knew that in their eyes, she was an oddity because she was only the second woman to be ordained as a rabbi in the United States. In the past a few such congregations had not taken her very seriously, but as the slender, twenty-seven-year-old brunette launched into her lecture, she decided that her misgivings had probably been unjustified. The audience seemed to be weighing her words quite carefully.

She told them that the time had arrived for Jewish women to assume a greater leadership role in the synagogue, and she argued that the masculine language of the liturgy should be changed. At the end of her talk Sandy threw the floor open to questions, and when she finally took her seat again, she was convinced she had succeeded in overcoming most objections her listeners had to giving Jewish women more power in their religious community.

But opposition materialized unexpectedly from another source. The Conservative rabbi who had introduced her—instead of just saying, "Thank you very much, Rabbi Sasso"—took the floor and argued against her points for a full twenty minutes. "Jewish history is not quite as bad as Rabbi Sasso has painted it," he said. "The role our women have played hasn't been so terrible either. She describes the position of our women in terms of a half-empty glass, but I would look at it as half full."

After he had stated a number of opposing arguments, he concluded by saying, "When Rabbi Sasso grows up, she'll change her mind and think a little differently about these things."

The members of the congregation were offended by these comments and many of them shook their heads in embarrassment. Sandy was outraged and didn't feel she could let the charges pass without an answer. Before the male rabbi could dismiss the congregation, Sandy got up again and said she felt his comments were "not balanced." She then restated a number of her points. Although she was quite upset with the man, she restrained herself because she knew from experience that "the less angry I appear, the more they accept me. People often have said they appreciate my not being militant or angry or hostile."

Sandy's experience is symptomatic of the inevitable frictions and resistances that accompany fundamental alterations in deeply ingrained religious customs. Women have traditionally occupied a secondary role in Jewish religious practice, and the notion of a female rabbi was a farfetched idea among most Jewish leaders a few years ago. But the winds of change for women in Judaism are blowing stronger every year, and tradition after tradition is being affected by the steadily increasing gale. Even the venerable sisterhoods that provide social and service outlets for lay women in temples and synagogues have been challenged. Rabbi A. James Rudin, Assistant Director of Interreligious Affairs for the American Jewish Committee, created a stir throughout the nation's Jewish communities in the summer of 1974 when he recommended that all the sisterhoods be disbanded. He argued that the organizations have "prevented women from moving into the mainstream leadership of synagogues" (*Jewish Journal*, June 21, 1974), but many rabbis and sisterhood members immediately took issue with him.

This reluctance to tamper with tradition can become especially entrenched when the tradition centers on Judaism's main repository of spiritual authority—the rabbinate. Sandy Sasso, a rabbi in the liberal

Reconstructionist movement, and Sally Priesand, the first female Reform rabbi and also the first Jewish woman to be ordained in this country (in June 1972), have both encountered hostility in their long, arduous path to the rabbinate. But their success in blazing new trails and setting solid precedents has made the road to spiritual leadership in Judaism a great deal easier for all women now than it was a few years ago.

Sandy decided when she was sixteen years old that she wanted to be a rabbi. It didn't cross her mind at the time that she was identifying with a role that was exclusively masculine. She had heard women read the Torah in her family's Reform synagogue in Philadelphia, but the only rabbis she knew were men. "In high school, rabbis I knew asked me to lead services for the youth group," she said. "They told me to write sermons for the young people, and I sometimes delivered them to the whole congregation. There wasn't any resistance in those congregations to my doing this sort of thing because I think they just wanted me to be involved as a young person in Judaism."

Sandy kept her career decision to herself at first, but finally she told her family rabbi. "He became very excited about it, and that was good for me because I suppose if there had been no encouragement I might have given up the idea," she said. "A lot of people thought it was kind of funny, a joke, something I would get over as I had gotten over other fads. But nobody discouraged me."

Sandy stuck by her decision and after she entered the Reconstructionist Rabbinical College in Philadelphia, she realized she wanted a congregation. She was drawn to the Reconstructionist tradition because of its emphasis on the preservation of Jewish peoplehood, without the supernatural dimensions of Conservative and Orthodox Judaism. Some of the traditional ceremonies and rituals, which have been discarded by liberal Reform Judaism, have been reaffirmed by the Reconstructionists, not as divine law handed down for all time from God to Moses, but as historical expressions of Jewish ideals. The flexible, open-ended attitude toward the law, or *halacha*, and toward the religious role of women in both the Reform and Reconstructionist movements paved the way for Sandy and Sally to be ordained as rabbis. The attitude of liberal Judaism toward women comes through clearly in a passage from an official pamphlet put out by the Jewish Reconstructionist Foundation: "Whereas Jewish tradition places women in a position of inferiority to men, as in the laws of marriage and divorce, Reconstructionism affirms that women must be recognized as equal to men in all matters of personal status." This affirmation of equality is followed by an approving reference to the trend toward the ordination of women as rabbis.

Orthodox and Conservative groups, who give more weight to tradition, have so far resisted the trend toward ordaining women, though, as we shall see later, harbingers of change have appeared on the Conservative horizon. The customary Jewish approach to women is reflected in a passage from a traditional prayer book in which men in the congregation say, "Blessed art Thou, O Lord our God, King of the universe, who has not made me a woman." The women, who apparently are not expected to be thankful that they are not men, merely respond, "Blessed art Thou, O Lord our God, King of the universe, who has made me according to Thy will."

Sandy Sasso married her husband, Dennis, who was also a Reconstructionist rabbinical student, after her first year of theological training. Until graduation she was listening to questions like this: "Are you going to teach in your husband's religious school?"

"How do you like that—a question like that after nine years of education!" she told Dennis in frustration. "I have the feeling a religious school is where people want me because I'm less threatening to them there."

This sort of question finally disappeared when she was hired as rabbi of the Manhattan Reconstructionist Havurah after her graduation in 1974.

Sally Priesand's journey to her present job as assistant rabbi of Manhattan's Stephen Wise Free Synagogue has been somewhat different, primarily because she has remained single. Like Sandy, Sally decided as an adolescent that she wanted to be a rabbi. She can remember thinking, "It's a ridiculous idea because there aren't any women rabbis." But fortunately, she recalls, "my parents didn't throw up their hands and say, 'What kind of job is that for a nice Jewish girl?' They said, instead, 'If that's what you want, you should do it.' They gave me a great deal of encouragement."

Unlike Sandy, Sally, a petite twenty-eight-year-old with long, abundant dark hair, has never had to counter the suggestion that she should teach in a husband's religious school. Instead, as an unmarried woman throughout her training at the Hebrew Union College-Jewish Institute of Religion in Cincinnati, she constantly faced this comment: "Well, she's just here to find a husband."

"I think I was accepted into the college because they never thought I'd actually become a rabbi," she said with a smile. "They thought I'd get married, and that would be the end of me."

But as the years passed, Sally began to look like a serious candidate for the rabbinate. As a result, one of the professors who opposed her aspirations to have a congregation approached one of her boy friends and said, "My boy, when are you going to do this school a favor? Marry her and get rid of her!"

As the only woman in the school and potentially the first female rabbi in the United States, her personal life sometimes resembled a goldfish bowl. "I didn't like it because everybody knew everything I did," she said. "Whoever I dated was always teased—people would say, 'Well, she's going to be the rabbi, so what are you going to be?' Some of the guys thought it was funny, but others couldn't take it. It was too threatening to them."

Her problems at seminary began early during the first year when she and her classmates were assigned to read in the chapel. "They assigned me the worst time a student could have to read—during exam week. The thing that especially bothered me was that the list for chapel was alphabetical for everyone except me. I heard from some other students that the professor who had made up the list forgot about me at first, so he put me on the end, in the middle of the examination period. I had to take seven exams in four days, and I preferred not having the responsibility of reading the service at that time because I didn't even live at the school. I knew I'd have to *schlep* all the way in just to be at the chapel. But even though I wasn't too happy about it, I didn't say anything."

Some of her fellow students came to the rescue, however. "They didn't think the arrangement was fair, so one of them traded with me, and I was able to read the service at another time. When I did finally read in the chapel, that was probably the first time everyone realized what I was doing at the school. I remember a professor walked in while I was in the pulpit and saw me and said, 'What's she doing up there? Is she a regular student here?'"

Sally found growing acceptance and support among her male classmates. She once overslept "for one of the most important tests of my life—the exam for the bachelor of Hebrew letters degree. I almost missed it. It's a five-part exam and was scheduled to begin at 8:30 A.M. One of my classmates called me at eight twenty-five and said, 'Where are you?'"

She cried, "Tell them I'm coming!" and threw her clothes on and got there just in time to take and pass the test.

A group of male students also taped lectures for her because she constantly traveled around the country speaking. "When I was ordained, my thirty-five classmates spontaneously stood up," she recalled. "That touched me very much because it showed the tremendous support they gave me and continue to give me. Only one of my professors refused to sign my ordination papers. I always knew he wouldn't do it. He didn't accept the concept of women in the rabbinate. But I think the professors were fair to me, even if they didn't all agree with the idea of a female rabbi."

The fight of both Sally Priesand and Sandy Sasso to gain acceptance as the first women rabbis in this country has not been limited to their seminary experience. Although Sandy has found a great deal of warmth and acceptance in the non-academic Jewish community, she has also encountered some reactions that have ranged from disbelief to outright hostility. One time when she called a doctor's office to make an appointment for herself, she told the nurse on duty, "This is Rabbi Sasso."

The nurse said, "Just a minute," and Sandy could hear the conversation behind the muffled phone. "There's a woman on the phone who says she's a rabbi!" said the startled nurse.

"It's possible," another nurse replied. "I've heard there are a few of them."

Then the first nurse came back to the phone and put Sandy down for an appointment. "I guess maybe she thought I was making a crank phone call, or something," Sandy recalled wryly.

But some of the reactions have been less accepting. "I got some publicity in seminary that provoked a woman to write me and say she had read that I was studying to be a rabbi," Sandy said. "She thought that was a terrible thing and said that although she usually closes her letters by wishing people success, she wasn't going to do that with me.

She hoped I'd study very hard and find that 'this is not what a nice Jewish girl should be doing.'

"This reaction is based partly on the fact that society is not yet ready to accept women in certain positions," Sandy said philosophically. "Also, women in Judaism have never been rabbis, and that makes it all the more difficult. They're ready to accept women as lawyers or doctors, but not in this role."

Sally Priesand, as we saw in a previous chapter, ran into a number of problems trying to find a congregation which would be willing to accept a woman rabbi. But when she finally settled on the Stephen Wise Free Synagogue in Manhattan, she found herself involved with a sympathetic Jewish community, and many of the problems she had confronted in seminary seemed to evaporate. The publicity that has surrounded her has even made her something of a celebrity. "I sign a lot of autographs," she said.

Once when she was at an airport, she handed her credit card to the reservations clerk, who studied it for a moment and asked, "Is 'rabbi' your first name?"

"No," Sally replied. "I *am* a rabbi."

A man standing nearby said, "Oh, I read all about you! Would you shake my hand?"

The only area in which she has found the members of her congregation hesitant to accept her is in officiating at funerals. "I don't think that's so unusual, though, because a time of crisis isn't a time to try to break down any social barriers," she said. "A person might say, 'My mother was traditional, so how could I have a woman rabbi at her funeral?' "

But even in this sensitive realm, Sally is gaining acceptance. Recently she was supposed to conduct a funeral, but the spokesman for the family said he didn't want to have a woman rabbi. The synagogue's chief rabbi told the man he would handle the ceremony, but then "five minutes later the man called back and said that he would take me, that he'd changed his mind," Sally remembered with a grin. "Probably his wife yelled at him."

Both Sandy and Sally have made headway in changing masculine pronouns and references in the worship liturgy and they have also instituted a few new rituals and customs which reflect a feminist orientation. Sandy, for example, often wears a *yarmulke,* or skullcap, during her worship services, even though this custom has usually been reserved for men. "Actually, there's no legal prohibition against a woman wearing the *yarmulke*," she said. "I'm breaking custom, but not any kind of religious law."

She has also established a new custom for female babies which is designed to give them the same introduction into the Jewish community that the *bris*, or circumcision rite, does for the male. This "naming ceremony," as she calls it, is performed in the couple's home. "There's no physical sign of the covenant as in circumcision, but we name the girl on the Sabbath so that the sign of the covenant becomes the Sabbath itself. Traditionally, the father was called to the Torah in the synagogue to name the girl, but the baby usually wasn't even present and the mother didn't do anything. That disturbed me because the experience the mother went through at birth was certainly as important as the father's. We've tried to include as much symbolism, warmth and festivity for the little girl as for the boy at his *bris*."

In the naming ceremonies over which Sandy has presided, the mother brings the baby forward to the rabbi, and both parents recite some statements Sandy has prepared about accepting the responsibility of raising the child. Then there is a special blessing to welcome the girl into the covenant, and the child is named in both English and Hebrew. The parents receive a certificate, patterned after other traditional Jewish documents, which states that on a certain date, their daughter has been initiated into the Jewish covenant. "May she grow into a service of good deeds," the document declares.

Then, as with the *bris*, the festivities begin. There is usually a table of cake and coffee and "a lot of joy and talking," Sandy said. "There is a great deal of laughter, and the parents have always said they feel very positive about the ceremony. That's the attitude we're trying to encourage, because we want to give the parents of the girl the same start as the boy's parents."

Sandy has also had a hand in changing traditional Jewish wedding ceremonies for women with a feminist orientation. One woman actually sought her out for the ceremony because of the fact that she was a female. "She thought a male alone wouldn't recognize some of her feminist concerns," Sandy said. "She requested that her mother find a woman rabbi, and they asked both Dennis and me to do it. She didn't want anything in the ceremony to say 'man,' so we had to use words like 'person' instead. The couple were committed to each other, but they wanted to stand on their own, not merge into one but share with each other. We wrote the wedding ceremony to reflect this attitude."

On another occasion, Sandy officiated at a wedding ceremony where the bride insisted on breaking a glass with her foot. In the traditional ceremony, only the man smashes the glass, to symbolize the tragic side of Jewish history.

Sandy's official presence at these weddings still amazes traditional Jews, who occasionally have to look twice when they hear the young woman with the stylish long brunette locks and model's figure is actually one of their ordained spiritual leaders. One bride's mother, in introducing Sandy to the wedding guests, kept stressing, "This is the rabbi—*really* the rabbi!"

Although Sandy and Dennis Sasso are rabbis of separate Reconstructionist congregations, they have found it's a decided advantage to be in the same field. They sometimes collaborate at home on presentations which they can each use in their respective congregations in Manhattan and Great Neck. During the 1974 High Holy Days, for example, Dennis noted that "we put a package of readings together and we each used it for our separate services."

"I had positive reactions in general to all those services," Sandy said. "Dennis and I picked some contemporary material for the readings and did some research on the concept of repentance, which is the primary theme of the High Holy Days. I gave a long presentation on the development of this concept at the first service. On each subsequent day I handed out some of the material which Dennis and I had prepared to the congregation so that they could deal in discussions with different aspects of the topic."

Sandy often departs from tradition in her services in that she relies on group discussions rather than sermons. "It's more difficult to give a short introduction and then lead discussions than it is just to lecture," she said. "It requires more tact and authority to control people's contributions so that everybody can participate."

But she admits that she's had some trouble being aggressive in controlling the direction of these discussions. "I've had difficulty in saying, 'Direct yourself to the point, you're going astray,'" she said. "I felt at first that everyone had a right to say what he wanted to say. 'These people come from good backgrounds and have a lot of knowledge, so why should I limit them?' I thought. If someone went on at length, I found it difficult to cut the person off. It was my youth, I think, because these people were quite experienced and learned, and I thought perhaps I shouldn't stop them. But now, I feel more comfortable saying, 'We have to move on to another topic,' or 'This is not what we're aiming at.'"

Some members of her congregation have criticized her discussion approach and have said they prefer sermons, but she counters, "Discussion and teaching are an important part of the service. Study is worship in Jewish tradition. I feel strongly about having discussion in the services, though I don't think sermons are necessarily a bad idea."

Besides collaborating on intellectual and theological problems, Sandy and Dennis also find themselves confronted with more mundane issues in their spacious Great Neck apartment. Dirty clothes and dusty floors are things that have to be taken care of regularly, and the question, as with married Christian pastors, is who does what? "We don't have a definite set of things each of us does, though I usually handle the heavy vacuuming and heavy cleaning," Dennis explains. "Laundry is fifty-fifty. We share the dishes, and I prepare the appetizer and salad—the non-cooking part of the meal."

One distinctive thing about their home life is that the Sassos have decided to keep a kosher home. "We started keeping a kosher house when we took over our congregations and moved to our apartment here on Long Island," Sandy explained. "We have many friends who are kosher and we wanted them to feel comfortable in our home."

"We have two sets of dishes—a dairy set and a meat set," Dennis said. "The glass dishes we have can be used interchangeably."

"It can get quite difficult, and it's more expensive to eat this way, but it's part of our identifying Jewishly," Sandy commented. "We grew up not living this way, and it was hard to adjust. But keeping kosher dishes is consistent for the Reconstructionist tradition. Reconstructionists emphasize Jewish customs and rituals as a means of identifying with the Jewish people. We don't conceive of it as a divine commandment handed down to us, though, so there's a lot of flexibility."

"Keeping a kosher home makes you conscious of your act of eating," Dennis said. "It elevates meals from the animalistic."

As the Sassos work out their peculiar domestic problems as the first rabbinical couple in the United States, Sally Priesand faces an entirely different set of personal challenges as the first single woman rabbi. An assertive young woman, she says one problem she encounters on dates is that "men are somewhat threatened by who I am and what I've accomplished. If I do marry, the man I marry will have to be very secure in his own position so that he will not feel threatened by all the publicity I get and all the things I'm expected to do because I'm the first [woman rabbi in the United States]. Also, he'll have to realize how much the rabbinate means to me and never ask me to give it up."

When a man she's dating is threatened by her, she says she "can just feel it, sense it, though it's difficult to put into words."

As for marrying another rabbi, she says, "I don't think I'd want to do that. I certainly had enough opportunity in seminary. There would be a tremendous amount of competition which I wouldn't want to get involved in. In the days before my consciousness was raised, I said that I'd only be my husband's assistant, that I'd never be above him. I certainly don't feel that way any more. I suppose it could work out if we were in two different congregations. I think it would be horrible to have to come home and talk about the same people if you had the same congregation. But if a man is secure in his position, it really doesn't matter to me if he's a rabbi or doctor or lawyer."

If she decides to marry, Sally doesn't think "there will be a problem of combining a career and a family. I've always said that in my synagogue there will be a nursery next to my study, and I'll take my kids along to work with me. On the other hand, if I don't get married, I don't think my life is going to fall apart. I'm very happy with what I'm doing, and I feel very satisfied and fulfilled."

The question of children has also confronted Sandy Sasso. When she was applying for jobs as a rabbi, one interviewer asked her, "Won't you be having children soon?"

Sandy realized that he was really asking, "Do you think you can handle all this—being a mother and a rabbi at the same time?" so she answered with a smile, "I won't have a child on Yom Kippur [the holiest Jewish ceremonial day, when the rabbi's duties are especially important], but maybe the day after."

Sandy, like Sally, plans to make her children fit into her career responsibilities, though she expects she would ask for a sabbatical just after a child is born. "I think having children could be an asset for me because the experience of childbearing and raising children would give me something I could contribute to congregation life," she said. "And I think it will work out because my husband expects to share in the raising of our child."

What's the outlook for other women who want to become rabbis? "I know a lot of Jewish women are getting interested in becoming ordained now," Sandy says. "The Reform and Reconstructionist movements are accepting women, and I think the Conservatives might. The latest position by the Conservatives said no, but I think they're waiting to see what will happen with the other Jewish groups. They admit women to Conservative seminaries to study, though not to be ordained. But they may ordain them eventually.

"I think women rabbis will be accepted as Hillel directors on college campuses, as teachers and as principals of religious schools. But it's most difficult for people to accept women as congregational rabbis. That will take a long time, even among the liberal congregations."

Sandy's observations are supported by recent news events, such as reports of increasing numbers of women in Reform and Reconstructionist seminaries. Also, the Conservative movement has been taking steps toward giving women a more equal status in its congregational structure. In the fall of 1973 the New York *Times* reported in a front-page story that the influential Committee on Jewish Law and Standards of the Rabbinical Assembly, the Conservatives' rabbinical body, had approved a resolution that women should be counted in the *minyan*, or ten-person quorum necessary for Jewish worship, which in the past was limited to males. The Conservative rabbis of each individual congregation still have discretion to follow or ignore this resolution, but the step is considered significant by experts on Jewish tradition.

Less than a year later, in another Conservative development, the president of the Rabbinical Assembly proposed that the Jewish

Theological Seminary of America—the leading school for training Conservative rabbis—should consider admitting women for ordination. In 1975, the new Assembly president predicted that "the question of entry of women into the Conservative rabbinate is not a matter of whether, but when."

"There's nothing in the Jewish law, or *halacha*, that says a woman cannot be a rabbi," Rabbi Sally Priesand argues. "It's been mostly a matter of tradition. A man's realm was the synagogue; a woman's realm was the home. Women were exempted from the various time-bound commandments so that they could be at home. They didn't have to pray three times a day, as the men of the community were expected to do, because they had to be around the house to raise the children. Raising children was as much a religious obligation for women as participating in the ritual aspects of the synagogue was for men. You could say the Jewish woman has been a second-class citizen, but she was honored and respected by Jewish tradition. And in ancient times, the Jewish woman had a higher position than women of other surrounding cultures.

"Women are still separated from men in very traditional Jewish worship services. The reasons given are that they are a source of distraction for a man—his mind is supposed to be on his praying, not on the woman sitting next to him. I don't know if that says something about the woman or the man. Then there are the laws of ritual purity, and the idea of the uncleanliness of the woman. Talmudic law says a woman can be one of the seven people who recite the blessings of the Torah. But they generally haven't been called up because, when a woman is having her period, she is considered unclean. She's not supposed to read from the Torah, and in order not to embarrass her, they just say she can never read. In Orthodox Judaism, men will never shake hands with a woman because they don't know whether she's clean or not.

"But in the Talmud, there is a statement that says, 'Words of Torah are not susceptible to uncleanliness.' As far as I'm concerned, that throws out the argument against women reading the Torah during their menstrual periods. You can find anything you want if you look hard enough in Jewish law. Many passages praise women, many scorn them. But all these passages were written by individual rabbis, and nobody knows what personal hang-ups drove them to make the statements they made."

Speaking of her own tradition, Reform Judaism, Sally says, "Women don't sit separately and are not obligated to follow all the laws of ritual purity. We don't accept the law in Reform Judaism. The beauty of the Reform tradition is that you decide for yourself which customs and ceremonies are to be meaningful to you."

But Orthodox Jews, who take the old religious laws, the *halacha*, quite seriously, have staunchly resisted these liberal interpretations of the ancient Hebrew code and traditions. They have continued to limit their *minyan*, or worship quorum, to males and have refused to consider seriously the ordination of female rabbis. "I don't think the ordination of women will happen in the Orthodox tradition, but at the same time, I'm not sure it should," Sally Priesand observes. "I happen to believe that all options should remain open. Those women who feel fulfilled within Orthodox Judaism should have that option, and if they need a more complete participation, they should go to the other traditions."

The role models that Rabbis Sally Priesand and Sandy Sasso have created for other young Jewish women seem destined to reinforce the feminist trend in liberal Judaism and result in the swelling of the ranks of female rabbis. One woman rabbinical student at the Hebrew Union College-Jewish Institute of Religion declared in a New York *Times* interview on May 26, 1974, that an article on Sally had reinforced her decision to apply for training as a rabbi. And when Sandy Sasso traveled up to Brandeis University in Massachusetts to give a lecture, she was picked up by a young girl who insisted on addressing her as "rabbi."

Sandy said, "Look, you can call me Sandy."

But the girl replied, "I just like to use the word because a *woman* is actually a rabbi. I want to become a rabbi myself, and it makes a difference that a woman has already gone through this."

"I think it makes a big difference that women can act as rabbis and other women can see them," Sandy said later. "Small children are the same way. If they don't see it happening, it doesn't exist. I went to one home where the parents have a small boy. Dennis was with me, and the parents introduced us and said, 'She's a rabbi too.' The boy looked at me for a moment, laughed, and said, 'No.'

"It struck me that it doesn't make any difference if someone tells you. If you're very young, you have to see it to believe it."

Sally and Sandy are there now for other young Jewish women to see, and believe, and inevitably to follow.

CHAPTER NINE

Rumblings
in the Roman Church

Father Brian Callahan, wearing a red plaid lumberjack shirt and old wash pants, dutifully donned an apron and walked into the kitchen in the rectory of St. Michael-St. Edward's Roman Catholic Church. He turned on the stove and started preparing the ingredients for his culinary specialty—veal scaloppine. With the same well-ordered precision he uses to conduct Sunday Mass, he set the table, whipped up a crispy salad and cooked the vegetables. Later that evening, he hurriedly whisked the steaming dishes out to the dining room and began serving the members of his "family"—the three nuns and two other priests who are part of a ministerial team in Brooklyn's low-income Fort Greene section. After the meal, as the sisters and other priests leaned back in their chairs and savored their coffee, Brian took charge of cleaning the table and popping the dishes in the dishwasher.

Father Callahan's domestic accomplishments are not the only departure from tradition in this inner-city parish. Tomorrow it will be Father George Wilders' turn to take over the kitchen. The next day Father Anthony Failla, who is the chief parish priest and also chairman of the Downtown Brooklyn Planning Board, will slave away over the stove. On succeeding evenings, the women—Sisters Georgianna

Glose, Sally Butler and Sheila Buhse—assume the cooking duties so that the men can enjoy a brief respite before their day of toil comes up again.

Under the watchful eye of Sister Georgianna, who has been elected to set up a work schedule, the nuns and priests in this topsy-turvy parish share equally in the rectory housework. And in the ultimate flaunting of Catholic tradition, these men and women not only rotate in the kitchen, but also take turns in speaking from the church pulpit, planning the Sunday liturgy and sitting the "duty" every day in the rectory.

"It's usually understood that when a Catholic wants to go to a rectory to talk about a religious problem, he'll be seen by a male priest," said Father Tony Failla, the big, broad-shouldered parish administrator who considers himself a co-equal team member. "But we realized that if we were sharing in other areas of our parish work, we should share in the duty as well."

This means that anyone coming to the rectory, whether it's to prepare for marriage or discuss a deep religious problem, has a fifty-fifty chance of seeing a nun instead of a priest. The first time Sister Sally Butler, a forty-three-year-old Dominican nun, answered the rectory doorbell, a male visitor on the doorstep looked past her and said, "I'd like to talk to a priest."

"I'm on duty today—what can I do for you?" Sally responded.

The man hesitated at first, then seemed to get his bearings and followed her inside.

"Some people were reluctant at first to tell me their problems," Sally said, "but usually they'd finally come out and say what they wanted."

Many times people who come to a rectory are facing a crisis and need not only counseling, but immediate action. Although the responsibility of becoming a community activist has in the past been regarded as mainly a "man's job," the nuns at St. Michael-St. Edward's have learned how to take charge of these tasks as decisively and competently as the priests. One distraught mother, for example, came to Sister Sally in tears after her teen-age son had been arrested by the police for robbery. Sally accompanied the woman to court and vouched for her son as a reliable person at the arraignment because the nun knew the family quite well. Then she put up bail for the boy from the church's bail fund.

"My point of view is this: whether I think he's guilty or not, I'm going to help this person as much as I can," Sally declared. "But there are times when I've refused to go to court because I know that the kid has been breaking the law repeatedly."

Wearing their full habits and appearing as the representatives of the church in these court cases, the nuns are able to double the official capacity of the parish to help those in trouble. "I've found that the judge is usually looking for someone who can help him out of this situation because in most cases he doesn't know what to do," Sally said.

During this court hearing, Sally "made a deal" with the judge, who decided to be more lenient with the youngster by releasing him in her custody. "Sister, can you arrange family counseling?" the judge asked. "Do what you can to work this thing out."

Sometimes she gets better results than the lawyer assigned to defend the youngster. "He may have a lawyer who doesn't even know his name," Sally says. "If the case is put off, he may have a different lawyer each time. I've often been to court eight or nine times with one person for a very simple thing."

The nuns and priests on duty also act as advocates for their parishioners by helping cut through bureaucratic red tape in city agencies. "We put pressure on government agencies to do the job they're supposed to," said Sister Sheila Buhse, who is the treasurer of a low-income housing co-operative. She encountered one elderly woman who had received a letter about Social Security which she couldn't understand. "She hid it in her drawer, hoping it would go away," Sheila said. "It simply required writing a letter to clear up the difficulty." Sheila wrote the letter for the woman and the problem was solved.

Although they had no prior experience in visiting and counseling parishioners, the nuns have also moved easily into this pastoral role. "In many ways, the sisters are more acceptable to people than the priests," says wiry, dark-haired Father Brian Callahan. "To many people, the image of the priest is one of detachment. He's the aloof single man, and celibacy isn't that easy to understand. So people think there's something mysterious about you since you're involved in the religious world. The sisters, on the other hand, have a warmth and a motherliness about them that we lack."

This motherliness makes the nuns a welcome sight among the tall, red brick housing projects in their largely black and Hispanic neighborhood. When the sisters walk down the streets of their "vertical parish," as they call it, people hang out of the windows and call down, "Sister! Come up and see the pictures of my grandson!" Or, "Come on up for a cup of coffee!"

"It's easy for a woman to go in and sit down with another woman who's all alone in her apartment," noted Sister Sheila, a thirty-eight-year-old, easygoing brunette. "There's no scandal if the two of us just sit there for two hours and gab with each other. That's one advantage we have over the priests."

The three nuns now fit naturally into the *de facto* role of women priests. But at the outset it wasn't too easy for them to adjust to the idea of a parish ministry and a quasi-communal life-style with men. Having had experience in religious education, they were originally invited to the parish with the idea that they would help the priests with children in the church. The most radical thing they did at that point was to move into their own apartment, but they stayed to themselves, ate their meals privately and were reluctant to try to blaze new trails of pastoral responsibility. Their reserved, passive approach to their new ministry can be traced to the cloistered lives they had led as traditional Catholic religious.

Prior to coming to St. Michael-St. Edward's, the sisters had spent their careers teaching in elementary and high schools and living in a highly structured monastic environment where conversation was permitted only at prescribed times. "All of us lived on a schedule of getting up at five-fifteen in the morning and getting to church for a 6 A.M. Mass," said blond, even-featured Sister Georgianna Glose, who has set up a telephone contact service for elderly shut-ins. At twenty-eight, she is the youngest member of the ministerial team. "When I first came here, sometimes I was up until two in the morning at community meetings. I certainly wasn't going to get up again at 5 A.M. This parish really shook our lives up."

Sister Sheila, who taught elementary and junior high school for eleven years, had problems adjusting to the freewheeling atmosphere of the Brooklyn parish when she arrived in 1967 with Sister Sally. "It was difficult for me not having a class to prepare for, or a group of kids to be ready to teach at nine every morning," she said. "The priests would say, 'Hang loose. The work will find you.' "

But not content to sit back and wait for people to come to her, she got more aggressive: she even began to go to the supermarket and "hung around the produce counter," just to meet people. "In the convent, we had been so task-oriented," she said. "Even our recreations in the evening were prescribed. We had to be either knitting or crocheting. God forbid if you enjoyed television! Out of the corner of your eye, you might be watching a plot unfold, but you always had to be doing something with your ten fingers." It took her at least a year to be able to "hang loose and relax," as the priests had advised.

It also took several months for the sisters to grow beyond their limited self-image as religious educators and regard the entire parish as their full-time responsibility. Living in a co-operative apartment two blocks from the church, the nuns at first met with the priests only once or twice a week to discuss how their respective programs were going. "We didn't even go to Sunday Mass here, believe it or not," said Sally. "We weren't parish-oriented. We'd go off to visit friends and attend their church."

Gradually, the nuns started attending the St. Michael-St. Edward's church and getting more involved in parish life. But their involvement remained limited. "The nuns did what you might call 'harmless work,' related to children and teen-agers," said Brian Callahan. "The priests still had control over the way things were run. They were the policy-makers, and they did the important things in the parish."

It wasn't until the original labor force of priests was depleted by staff changes that the nuns and priests grew together as a team. "The two priests who were left were eating alone in the rectory at night, and we scurried over to our apartment just to cook for each other," Sheila recalled. "Sister Sally and I decided, 'This is silly!' Someone finally suggested, 'Why don't we all eat together?' "

As they began to take their meals together, ideas about how to improve the parish began to be tossed back and forth at the table. Soon, the women began sharing the decision-making with the men. They discussed the liturgy and the physical needs of the church. Then they began to talk about shifting the women's focus in the parish from children to the family and to the problems of elderly people in the community.

A year later, Tony, George and Georgianna arrived at the parish, and the new concept of the team ministry took shape. The focal point of this ministry is the nightly communal meal which symbolizes the egalitarian life-style which has evolved in the parish. "We are here to serve this community," Brian says. "Sharing food, cooking and serving each other is a visible sign of how we do it." Then he adds with a twinkle, "We have more cookbooks than theology books."

The significance of the Brooklyn experience and similar experiments in other Roman Catholic parishes may be profound if these ideas and practices continue to spread. "We've reversed the whole theology of going to church to share bread and wine, the Lord's Supper, together," Brian explains. "We don't believe that's the important thing. We believe that it's only important if you are sharing food and drink together in a sense of community and fellowship in your own home. That's the religious act."

Although the priests and nuns at St. Michael-St. Edward's look upon their evening repast as a vital, inspiring time together, more traditional clergymen sometimes find it difficult to accept the notion of sharing the dinner table with nuns. A young priest who knew the group well was having lunch with a fifty-year-old priest when the conversation turned to the Fort Greene parish. The younger clergyman asked, "Why don't you go down there and have dinner with the priests and sisters? You'll really enjoy yourself, and they'd like to have you."

The older priest looked shocked and inquired, "Do the sisters eat at table down there?"

"Sure," replied his companion.

"I can't take that at all," the older man said.

Many priests and nuns have been segregated by function and lifestyle for so long that they sometimes feel uncomfortable in each other's company at social gatherings. But the Brooklyn team has moved to break down these barriers. Father Brian Callahan put some of his fellow priests on the spot when he showed up at a "clerical stag party" with dark-haired Sister Sally, displaying her most radiant smile. Some of the priests were very solicitous and tried to make the nun feel at home. "Others were stunned," Sally said. "They didn't know what to do with me."

After getting her plate of food at the buffet, she made it a point to stand up until someone asked her to sit down. One priest, sitting by an empty chair, didn't budge, even though Sally was standing right in front of him. Finally, another priest came over and asked her to join him.

"I never did get upstairs," Sally said with a laugh, referring to an all-male discussion session on the second floor. "I found out later they were having a conversation about nuns."

"The priest's reaction depends on the individual," explained Father George Wilders, one of the team members, who runs a community credit union. "Sometimes priests just aren't accustomed to having a woman around. They are used to clerical stag parties, which are a cultural thing in many parishes."

One of the most valuable contributions of the sisters to the life of the parish has been in the liturgy. "After the priority of the parish changed from children to families, we realized we had only one time when people were our captive audience—that was during the Sunday services," said Georgianna. "Sunday was our time to use the Word of God to teach them as much as we could. That's where our expertise in education came in."

The nuns applied their knowledge of audio-visual teaching aids and curriculum planning, and the Sunday service became a vehicle for adult education as well as a worship experience. The priests and nuns now take turns each week preparing the liturgy and the homily. The man or woman in charge assigns roles in the service to the other members of the team.

"The only thing the women don't do is consecrate the sacred elements [during the Eucharist] and absolve in confession," said Father Tony Failla. "We are not at that point yet in the church."

Usually the traditional Catholic liturgy is rewritten at St. Michael-St. Edward's to fit the educational needs of the congregation. "We need to impart certain basic information, such as who were the apostles, and who was Paul," Sister Sheila said. "To get these points across, we rearrange the readings into a chronological sequence and rewrite some of the prayers. We also highlight certain days that are especially important to our parishioners, like Mother's Day and Thanksgiving."

The theme of the service is simplified to the point that it can be stated in one sentence so that the message will be absolutely clear to the congregation. At the 1975 New Year's service, which was conceived and directed by Sister Sally, the theme of the worship was hope. When the parishioners arrived, they were seated on benches which the team had arranged around a circular table in the rear of the church. The only object on the table was a blank slate. The lights were dimmed, and music swelled in the background. One of the priests who had been assigned to his role by Sally came out and explained in English and Spanish that the clean slate was a symbol of the new year ahead. "It was a difficult year for all of us as a nation and as a parish," he said. "But there are so many reasons for hope." The prayer and Bible reading which followed also focused attention on this overriding theme of hope. Then the priest repeated the theme in another short talk.

"This may seem like a lot of repetition, but we find it's necessary," Sally said. "People don't always listen the first time."

Using visual concepts from her educational training, Sally next arranged for some slides to appear on a giant screen which was hanging behind the altar. The first ten pictures were a grim reminder of the woes of 1974, including scenes of starving people and the Watergate scandal. Then, as gospel music started to play, the parishioners were treated to sixty shots of happy times in the parish. There were photos of recent weddings and baptisms, the police department's judo demonstration for the senior citizens, and the fire truck and firemen that came to the memorial service for the people who had died in fires in the community.

After a brief meditation, the congregation got up and walked to one side of the church for a fellowship with punch and cookies, prior to the Mass. When the time arrived for the Eucharist, the two hundred congregants moved to the front of the church. There, the priests in their vestments broke bread before the church's rugged altar, which is made out of railroad ties from the old elevated train tracks.

With the new emphasis on teaching during the Sunday services, the team members find it necessary to evaluate their performances during the weekly staff meetings Monday morning. "We review what we did the day before to learn from it so we don't make the same mistakes again," Tony said. Under the old system, where the priests merely recited a standard liturgy and presented a brief homily, "the only negative feedback was that people might not come to church," he said. "Now we feel open enough to share with each other by criticizing such things as the length and content of the homily."

After this Monday meeting, the weekly routine of this unusual parish begins again as the priests and nuns hop into one of their cars and head toward a local market to buy the week's groceries.

Although many grass-roots reforms in the Catholic Church are taking place in parishes like St. Michael-St. Edward's, a cloud of potential dissension and even schism lurks on the horizon. That cloud is the same one that has caused storms of controversy in the Episcopal Church—the issue of women's ordination. Nuns are lay women, and that status bars them from the exclusive male club of priests, which is the center of ecclesiastical power. Sister Sally Butler is in many ways equal to her three parish priests, but she was relieved of any illusions about her position in the church as a whole when Father Brian Callahan took her to that clerical stag party. Although the priests there were mostly polite, they were not ready to accept her fully as a member of their club because as a woman she lacked that necessary qualification of membership: ordination.

Sally, for one, would like to become a priest so that the matter would be laid to rest. "I don't like to see the inequality that exists right now," she says. "I think it's foolish, and the sooner it's over, the better. For that reason, I would like to see the ordination of women, and I would like to be ordained. But I'm not going to waste any time crying, and I'm happy in what I'm doing. I feel that what I'm doing is priestly."

Sister Sheila Buhse, on the other hand, doesn't care whether she's ordained or not. "Whether I have the title or not doesn't really bother me," she says. "We see priesthood differently here. It's not just liturgical; it's ministering to people where they are in this time and place in history. You can already call us priests in that sense. I'm satisfied with my work and with the response of people to us."

"I think ordination would be a step backward," Brian declares. "The ordination of religious women would just add to a clericalism that we hope is passing."

But what chance will women have to exercise power in the church and make their voices and opinions heard if they're not ordained?

"Priestly functions are not as important as we once thought," Brian responds. "And our emphasis on the sacredness of everything—of secular life, community life, political life—has made the priestly function a much wider thing than we ever dreamed of ten years ago."

"Ten years ago, it would have been essential that women be ordained priests," agrees Father Tony. "Today, it's not even that important that *men* be ordained priests. What we're working toward is a new understanding of what religious people do. We're going to come up with something that is new."

As Sister Georgianna explains it, the new concept of priesthood that is being evolved, not only in the Brooklyn parish but throughout the Catholic Church, is tied to the notion of the priesthood of the laity which was enunciated at the Second Vatican Council. "More and more, the whole idea of priesthood is not in one person," she says. "It's not just a few people giving service to the community—but everyone. Every Catholic is called to be a priest in the sense that he is called to give service and to make God present to his family, his neighbors and his community."

These words seem strangely reminiscent of some of Martin Luther's arguments about the priesthood of the believer which split the church centuries ago. Skeptics might argue that it's a pipe dream to think such revolutionary concepts of ordination could ever prevail in the Roman Catholic hierarchy, but the nuns and priests in Fort Greene are pushing ahead with practical applications of their ideas. They have created a special "ordination" ceremony for people in the parish who have dedicated themselves to serving others. Designated as "ministers of special service," these parishioners are "recognized as ministers by the people of the parish," says Father George Wilders. "And they are really sharing in the ministry of the parish."

The special ministers include two women who are involved in community work, a woman who is devoted to helping the elderly, and three people who contribute their musical talents to the church. Although some might argue that this recognition of lay people is just another version of the concept of the lay minister, or "extraordinary minister," which is a well-established Catholic program, Father Brian

Callahan insists "we give it a different theological nuance. We've made it something which is on a par with our ministry."

Despite the innovations that the nuns are helping to institute at St. Michael-St. Edward's, they are still quite conscious of and obedient to the authority and tradition of the Roman Catholic Church. They don't regard themselves as religious subversives in any sense. "We don't deny our heritage," Sister Sally says. "We're only as effective as we are because church authorities have blessed us," added Father Tony Failla.

Although the Brooklyn team is optimistic that a new order is coming in the Catholic Church, and the women argue categorically that "this is the best time in the world to be a religious man or woman," not all Catholic women are so satisfied. Frances L. McGillicuddy, a retired New York City schoolteacher, has been fighting for women's ordination since the early 1960s. The founder of the United States Section of the St. Joan's International Alliance, a lay movement for women's rights, Frances is skeptical of the willingness of women—especially nuns—to take on a ministerial role without pressing for ordination.

"The church doesn't want to ordain women as deacons or as anything else," she says bluntly. "Instead, they tell women, 'You are ministers by virtue of your baptism. You don't have to be a priest in order to serve.' A lot of nuns buy that argument," she says.

As she sees it, these nuns are in effect serving in "mini-ministries," which still have second-class status in the eyes of lay people and of the church.

The feisty Frances believes the priesthood will never be opened until women start badgering their bishops and the Vatican. Her eyes twinkle as she reveals one of her tactics: During the height of her arguments with opponents of ordination, she sometimes flashes a row of belligerent buttons which are pinned to the inside of her suit jacket. The slogans proclaim: "Equal Rites for Women," "No Mini-Ministries," and "Women, Don't Make Coffee! Make Policy!"

She advocates that lay women and nuns start putting pressure on their parish priests by refusing to work until the priest recognizes the equality of women. One example she cites is a woman from Connecticut who had been a leading Sunday school teacher in her parish for years. When the woman asked her priest to appoint her as a lector—a special position for lay Scripture readers—he refused.

"In that case, I won't keep teaching Sunday school," she told him defiantly.

"That's blackmail," he said. But when the woman started to follow through with her threat, the priest relented and named her to the post.

Frances and her supporters are willing to wage an uphill battle for equality within the church even if the ultimate goal of priesthood is in doubt. But other women are not so patient. Two female Roman Catholic chaplains at the Harvard-Radcliffe Student Center in Cambridge, Massachusetts, are getting out of church work because they see no home for women in the Catholic ministry. The chaplains, Sister Ann Kelley, a Dominican nun from Illinois, and Carole Bohn, a lay minister who is qualified to perform certain pastoral and worship functions, both adamantly reject the priesthood as a suitable goal.

"Priesthood in the Roman Catholic Church is a very exclusive male club with its own prerogatives and privileges," says blue-jean-clad Ann, as she brushes her long red hair away from her face and gestures with a lighted cigarette. "Priests exert a lot of power over people's lives in a negative way. I would prefer that any authority I might have would be merited by me and not by my office."

Carole, a low-keyed thirty-two-year-old with long, flowing black hair, agrees. "I can see a great many reasons in my work here why ordination would be an advantage," says Carole, who holds a master of divinity degree from the Harvard Divinity School. "But I also know so many ordained people who are under the grip of authority. I would not want to trade my freedom for the authority of ordination. If the system were to change, then I would want to be ordained."

What Carole envisages is "real involvement of the laity in the government of the church," a step which she believes is far from being realized. Carole's and Ann's disaffection with the church hierarchy and their pessimism in general about ordination stem in part from the fact that they are leaving their chaplaincy jobs under less than happy circumstances. They have been relieved of their posts, and although the precise reasons for their dismissals were never made clear, they have a few speculations.

"We tried to represent a different kind of church, a non-clerical church, which the authorities might not have regarded as particularly orthodox," Carole said. As an example, she explained that although she has never had occasion to advise a student who wanted an abortion, her approach in such counseling situations would diverge from what would be considered the traditional Catholic position. "Personally, I would want to bring the woman to the point of making her own decision, and support her in that decision, whatever it might be," Carole explained. "Anyone who was trying to adhere to the position of the church would not do that. Traditionalists would try to convince the person that her only choice was to have the child."

In addition to such an unconventional counseling approach, the fact that Carole conducted a series of Catholic services in one of the buildings in Harvard Yard was also, on occasion, the source of controversy. One morning she handled the entire first part of the service, known as the "liturgy of the Word." The liturgy opened with a penance, where Carole asked the 130 students in the congregation to confess their sins of the week. She then gave them priestly absolution: "May Almighty God forgive us, have mercy upon us, and grant us the life everlasting." Carole was unaware that two young women in the congregation were whispering to one another with stern expressions.

After readings from the Epistles and the Gospels, Carole launched into her homily on the topic of world hunger. The previous week, she had participated in a student fast to raise money for organizations working with the hunger problem, so she had plenty of firsthand information. During the brief sermon she talked about the Christian responsibility to help and criticized the "triage," or selective starvation, plan which had been suggested by some specialists as a solution. Then she opened the floor for discussion before the priest conducted the Communion service.

As Carole was leaving the building after the service, a male student stopped her and said, "I think you should know something: I was talking with two girls just now who were in the congregation, and they were very upset about the whole thing. Even though a priest handled the Eucharist, they didn't think that you, as a woman, should be conducting that much of the worship service."

"I think it's unfortunate they didn't feel they could come and tell that to me," Carole replied.

Although Carole received more positive than negative responses to her worship leadership, she and Ann have had some disagreeable personal experiences that have hardened their resolve to steer away from ordination. Ann, for example, believes many priests she has dealt with try to assume a role that makes them superior to others. The Harvard-Radcliffe Catholic Student Center is an accredited field education project for students at a Jesuit theological seminary in Cambridge, and the women often have had to supervise the counseling training of young Jesuit priests, some of whom fit into a mold as "little superclerics," to use Carole's words.

"We sent one guy over to have supper with some freshmen students at Harvard," said Ann. "He came back and said he'd go somewhere to eat later but he wouldn't eat there because he had to stand in line. He thought he was exempt from the rest of the world."

Another reason that ordination seems less attractive to Carole is that she has found that she can be more effective sometimes in counseling situations because of her lay status. One evening a frazzled middle-aged woman came to the chaplains' office looking for the priest who works with the two women. Since Carole was sitting alone in the lounge, the woman tearfully poured out the story to her.

"It was kind of natural for us to begin talking," Carole said. She soon learned that the woman was the mother of a girl whom Carole and a priest had been counseling for marriage. "The mother was very upset about something related to the marriage," said Carole, who did not indicate to the woman that she was familiar with the situation.

After an hour's conversation, the woman said gratefully, "Gee, it's been really good talking to you. I never thought of the possibility of talking to a woman. It's so much easier to talk to a woman than to a man. You know, you really ought to go into counseling."

"That's why I'm a chaplain here," Carole said.

"Oh!" exclaimed the startled woman. "I thought you were a secretary!"

Carole evaluates the woman's attitude this way: "Because I wasn't a priest, she related to me as another human being—another woman—not as some person fulfilling a role."

There are times, however, when a person in distress wants the security of turning to a priest, and that's why the priesthood remains the ultimate objective of some Catholic women. Nancy Kehoe, a lively thirty-seven-year-old nun from Chicago, became painfully aware during one counseling situation that the fact she was not ordained created a barrier which could never be surmounted. After Nancy had spent two months counseling a geriatric patient in the psychiatric ward of a mental hospital, the woman turned to her and said, "I'd really like to go to confession now."

Nancy was struck speechless. "I had to bring in a token priest for two minutes to hear her confession when I'd really been hearing it for the past eight weeks. She couldn't accept the fact that I could forgive her, and in terms of the church's understanding of the sacrament, I *couldn't* forgive her."

This incident was the turning point for Nancy in making her actively seek the priesthood as a goal. "I said to myself, 'This is for the birds! I should be able to do that.' "

Instead of taking a militant stance, however, the witty, unaffected Sister Nancy is approaching the priesthood pragmatically. With a Ph.D. in counseling psychology, the former high school teacher "zeroed in" on the field of spiritual direction and retreat work, an area in which women can work effectively without ordination. "It's like being a spiritual guru," Nancy explained, "or someone who helps others develop their relationship with God and a life of prayer."

Nancy believes that it's "important that women be trained along those lines instead of just accepting the authority of men in the church to do this work." Many times, she says, priests are not trained to handle specialized counseling problems. In the past, people thought these special skills were "just part of the totality of blessings that the priest was supposed to be endowed with at ordination." But when Catholic authorities realized many men are not so endowed, the field became wide open for trained women.

After a year of training at Weston School of Theology in Cambridge, Massachusetts, Nancy accepted an offer to be the first woman faculty member at the Jesuit school. She decided that "if women were ever going to be ordained, then the first step would be for seminaries to give them faculty recognition and training."

Weston was a "foot in the door" of the priesthood for Nancy. "Only a place like a Jesuit school, which is free of the archbishop's power grasp, could possibly give women proper training and then play an advocacy role to see that they get ordained," she said.

Within a year of joining the Weston faculty, Nancy opened the door for female church leadership a little wider by speaking up for women's rights. At one faculty meeting, to which the religious superiors of the students in the school were invited, Nancy looked around the room and realized she was the only woman present. Although there were several different orders of religious women in the school, none were represented by their superiors.

Before the discussion got under way, Nancy piped up: "I find it very interesting that none of the orders of religious women are represented."

The men were dumbfounded. "It was as if I had asked them to strip," said Nancy, laughing as she recalled the incident. "Unless a woman is present, that kind of question never comes up. It's not ill will on the part of the men. They simply don't think of it."

As a result of Nancy's pointed comment, the school arranged to hold a special meeting with the superiors of several women's orders. "I see my role now as raising that kind of question so that if the men are serious about giving women seminary training, they'll see all the ramifications of that issue," she said.

Ultimately, though, Nancy is pinning her hopes for the priesthood on the possibility that the diaconate will open to women. Although there were female deacons in the early church, women have not been admitted to the diaconate for centuries. "If they restore the diaconate, they are in fact restoring the concept of ordination to women," Nancy says.

Recently, the church allowed married men to move into a permanent diaconate to meet the manpower demands of the church. Although the priesthood is presently closed to the men who choose this option, some people, like Father George Wilders of the Fort Greene parish, think that it won't remain closed for long. "If you have married men being ordained deacons, it's only a matter of time before the church will ordain married men as priests," he says.

Most observers agree, however, that the celibacy requirement for male priests, which is based on culture, tradition and history rather than on theology, will have to be eliminated long before women are admitted to the priesthood. Part of the reason is political: "If they started letting women into power positions in the church, some of the men would lose their power," says Sister Nancy Kehoe. Masculine power concepts are deeply ingrained in the system so that nuns are taught to "look to priests as the ultimate resource," says Nancy. "In the church, sisters have really put priests up on a pedestal. Father knew best and had all the answers."

Male priests are an ultimate resource, not only for decisions, but often for economic needs as well. Several years ago, Sister Nancy counseled a nun who was the principal of a school. "She had to ask the pastor for stamp money," Nancy said. "That's real oppression as far as I'm concerned."

But power is not the only threat that women pose for the priesthood, in the opinion of some churchwomen. "Women personally are threatening to a man's celibacy," said Sister Ann Kelley. "Because the hierarchy, the entire clerical world, is completely celibate, their attitudes about women have been peculiar. I think that they don't know much about women, really. There's a recurrent thread in their thought that women are dangerous—that they are temptresses and sirens."

Sister Nancy Kehoe sees women as a threat to the sexual identity of priests, whose male self-concepts are sometimes linked to the notion that the priesthood is a distinctively male role. "If women can become priests, what does this mean for the men?" she asks. "Many of them haven't really defined priesthood for themselves. Often, they got into it at an early age and just accepted the fact that they were priests, without asking themselves what it meant."

One young Jesuit in training for the priesthood was very hostile to Harvard chaplain Carole Bohn, who was his supervisor in pastoral work. After several weeks of blistering encounters, he finally admitted, "I think part of the reason I can't relate to you as a supervisor is because you're a woman. The only time I ever had women in positions of authority over me was when I was in grade school."

Despite the resistance Catholic women are meeting in their fight for positions of leadership, Father Brian Callahan, of Brooklyn's St. Michael-St. Edward's, is optimistic. He thinks that the days of the authoritarian power that holds women back in the Roman Catholic Church are numbered. "I think the whole issue of ordination of women is tied to whether there will be a continuation of the male priesthood," he said. "We are all laity before we are anything else— because of our baptism. And if we emphasize that, and de-emphasize the unfortunate historical development of the male priesthood, we get back to our real emphasis—which is equality.

"I feel that's the way the Spirit is leading the church. We are shifting toward democratization, toward a view of ministry where *each* Christian has a sense of ministry."

And in his Brooklyn parish, the Spirit does seem to be moving to open up the minds of both the men and the women in the pastoral team. "Women can be called to the ministry only when men are no longer threatened by their presence," says Sister Sally Butler. "We've experienced that here. The men have found they're not lacking in maleness just because we're doing what they have traditionally done."

Perhaps the next few years will tell whether the Brooklyn experience is just an ephemeral phase in the church's history or a harbinger of change that will move through the American hierarchy and reach to the very foundations of Catholicism in Rome.

CHAPTER TEN

Filled with the Spirit

Diane Pierce was ready for bed. She fluffed her rich, wavy brown hair, took off her glasses and sighed deeply. As the youthful pastor of a historic Connecticut Congregational church, she faced many pressures and concerns each day as she tended to the needs of her congregation. An argument with some of her church leaders that afternoon had made her especially tired this evening—so tired that she knew that her daily time of meditation was even more important than usual.

She knelt before a small altar she had arranged on one side of her bedroom, lit a candle and assumed a yoga position. To further quiet her mind, she took a rosary and began to murmur a prayer, "Lord Jesus Christ, have mercy." She repeated the prayer, like a Christian mantra, around the rosary. After a half hour of such prayers and yoga exercises, Diane, a prim, reserved New Englander, felt calm enough to meditate even more deeply and listen for God to speak.

Then the familiar physical feeling came upon her—"wham! Like a wave coming over me with such tremendous force that I was left all shaky." When Diane enters one of these states, she says, "my palms get wet, my throat gets dry, my heart begins to pound." She reached for a nearby pen and spiral notebook and began to write down "like dictation" the revelation she felt she was getting from the Lord.

"You say you want to do great things for me here," she wrote. "I say to you that you can do nothing. You are helpless. You are totally useless to me as you are. You must die. You must cease to exist as Diane Pierce and begin to exist as a reflection of Christ before you are of any use to me at all. You must breathe for me and walk for me and talk for me. But it must not be you breathing and walking and talking, but me breathing and walking and talking inside of you. Do you understand that?

"I will make you understand. I will tell you a mystery. No great thing shall be done in that church until you love [the church leaders you argued with today] from your heart. I have sent you to feed my sheep, but you have judged them instead and found them wanting. You have vaunted yourself up and grown proud in your spirituality, and you are hindering me. I want you to repent. I want you to sit in sackcloth and ashes before me and humble yourself and begin anew to learn of me and to trust me. I want you to work and pray until you can love every member of this congregation, and then I want you to thank me for taking away from you everything you want. You are *my* servant, remember that! I do to you what it pleases me to do, and I will not be judged by anyone!"

After this revelation, Diane said she felt "like I'd been hit in the stomach." She realized that she would have to follow the direction she felt God had given her. The next morning, she got in touch with a young woman who was a close friend and a member of her congregation. "I talked to her about the revelation and said I knew I had been proud," Diane recalled. "We had both been making fun of the other people in the church, judging them, saying they were stupid about some spiritual things. We decided that the Lord had called us for repentance. My friend said she felt there was as much for her in that revelation as for me. It was in a sense a prophecy to another person. We asked the Lord to forgive us and show us what he wanted us to do. We finally resolved not to talk about the people in the church any more, and I started praying that the Lord would show me how to love them."

Diane has experienced a number of personality conflicts with the lay leaders of her congregation, partly because of the fact that she's the church's first woman pastor. But she finds answers to her problems and constant spiritual nurturance in these direct divine revelations, or "prophecies" as she calls them. Many other female pastors have also found that a deep faith in God is the central factor in their ability to overcome the tensions and pressures that naturally accompany their trend-setting careers in a male-dominated profession. When they run into problems on the job—such as hostile lay people or snubs from male pastors—they fall back on prayer, on a personal relationship with God. The answers to these prayers may involve concrete happenings in the congregation, such as a change in a hostile attitude, or an inner sense in the minister that a certain course of action is correct. And this inner conviction or the feeling that God is helping out, leading the pastor through tough situations, can be a source of great power and a great antidote to anxiety and confusion. Diane's experience is especially striking and dramatic because she has developed an almost mystical relationship with God. Her present spiritual orientation began with her initiation into the charismatic or neopentecostal movement which has been making inroads during the last decade in most Protestant denominations and also many Roman Catholic churches.

"I'm a very cautious person, not easily swept off into things," Diane says. "The Lord sometimes has to hit me over the head to wake me up. I was getting depressed with my performance with my congregation, and an Episcopal man I knew said, 'What you need is the Holy Spirit.' I didn't know much about the Holy Spirit because that's not a doctrine that's emphasized much in the Congregational Church." Her friend explained briefly about the "baptism of the Spirit," a spiritual experience stressed by pentecostals which results in such gifts as speaking in tongues (glossolalia), faith healing, prophecy and a generally deepening commitment to a more spiritual life-style. This baptism of the Spirit is often accomplished during an independent "laying on of hands" ceremony by other pentecostals after the Christian's initial baptism with water.

Diane's friend put his hands on her head and prayed that God would give her the Spirit. "But I wasn't in the mood," Diane said. "I felt uncomfortable and it was terribly threatening. He kept telling me to praise the Lord in tongues, but I couldn't do it. I wanted to with all my heart, but something was blocking me. It seemed stupid, offensive to me in a way. I suppose I really didn't want to do it."

She began to cry and finally went home "with the feeling that nothing had really happened." But she was still interested in having this experience, so she decided to attend a seminar on the "baptism of the Spirit" with some Yale University people in New Haven. After the seminar, Diane went to a meeting with about forty other people—lawyers, nurses, Yale professors—who had jammed into a private living room in New Haven. She and her fellow seminar students were prayed over by others, and the experience was something she'll never forget.

"The other seminar people started jumping up and shouting, 'Praise the Lord!' and singing and praying in tongues," she said. "They were all crying and laughing, but absolutely nothing happened to me. I just sat there like a bump. More and more people walked over to pray over me, and I finally just asked them to stop. My friends were so disappointed in me, and everybody was embarrassed."

Diane ran into the kitchen and cried. A Catholic nun followed her in and tried to comfort her, but she said she felt "absolutely humiliated." During the ride home that evening, she sensed her friends were angry at her.

"You're egotistical, Diane!" one said accusingly. "The Holy Spirit is trying to work through you, but your ego won't let you speak in tongues. Why are you fighting the Lord?"

She didn't have an answer at the time, and she was thoroughly depressed when she shut her front door behind her that night. But she began to pray, and she sensed that God was answering by saying, "You're a fool, Diane! You've already been baptized in the Spirit [by the Episcopalian]. What's the matter with you, that you don't trust me? Look at all the things I've done for you lately."

As she began to mull over this thought, she realized that some interesting things *had* been happening to her since her Episcopalian friend had first laid his hands on her head and prayed over her. "I had had a chronic stomach problem all through college, and it had given me agony," she said. "I kept getting sick, and when I entered Mount Holyoke College, it went haywire. I passed out on the street once, hit my head on a parking meter and was in the hospital with a concussion for a week. But suddenly, I realized that evening that it was gone. My stomach had healed after that first spiritual baptism experience. I had also been grossly overweight before the baptism, but I had dropped from a size 16 to a size 12 dress. The pounds had really melted away."

So she began to feel more positive about her spiritual condition and also sensed something was pulling her back to that group in New Haven. She returned to their next meeting, "but I sat in a corner, where nobody could see me," she said. "The others sat around on the floor. Close to the beginning of the meeting, they had what they call a 'singing in the spirit,' where somebody just begins to sing in tongues. If you feel like it, you join right in. No two people have the same tongue, but somehow they harmonize. It has to be the Holy Spirit—otherwise you'd think it would sound like bedlam."

She had no intention of trying to participate with the group that night, and she was so inconspicuous over in her corner that she felt safe. "But I found I really wanted to sing. I opened my mouth and started to sing in tongues, and I spoke in tongues that night too. I've been able to do both ever since."

Diane describes her glossolalia as having a "guttural" sound and notes that "there's a difference between singing and speaking in tongues. The singing is spooky—like a kind of Indian flute. It's funny, because my dogs recognize it. When I get into bed, they'll get on it with me, hang over the edge, sigh, and go right to sleep. The sound seems relaxing. The same thing happens with babies. I've put babies to sleep singing in tongues over them. I took this one baby who was crying out for a walk, and as a last resort I started singing in tongues, and she went right to sleep."

Diane usually speaks in tongues when she feels some prompting from God. "It's a great release. It doesn't involve supplication on my part. It just comes over me. The Lord will say, 'Why don't you speak to me in tongues?' I can feel the tensions draining away from me when I do it. I'll go for several days or a week without doing it, and then do it for several days in a row. There's no rhyme or reason to it. I've told my parishioners about my experience with the Spirit in general terms, but I haven't mentioned the tongues except to a small group. The majority of the congregation seems to accept me as a sort of religious fanatic," she added wryly.

Her spiritual life seems to encompass elements of traditional mysticism, as William James described it in his *Varieties of Religious Ex-*

perience. James enunciated several classic "marks" of mystical experiences: ". . . mystical states are more like states of feeling than states of intellect . . . They are states of insight into depths of truth unplumbed by the discursive intellect . . . illuminations, revelations, full of significance and importance . . . they carry with them a curious sense of authority for aftertime . . . half an hour; or at most an hour or two, seems to be the limit beyond which they fade into the light of common day . . . the mystic feels as if his own will were in abeyance, and indeed sometimes as if he were grasped and held by a superior power."

Because Diane is a product of the contemporary charismatic movement, certain other distinctive traits characterize her spiritual life. In addition to speaking in tongues, she has even been exorcised twice, though she regards both of these experiences with some skepticism. In one meeting with the charismatic group in New Haven, she told them she was upset about a big blow-up she had just had in her church.

"Satan has got into you," one fellow said. "Satan's depressing you."

He told her to kneel on the floor, and the others surrounded her and put their hands on her head and began to pray in tongues and commanded Satan to come out. "In the name of Jesus Christ, I command you to come out of her!" a man kept shouting.

Diane said she "had a sense of peace afterward, but I think it was because I got sympathy for my problem."

Other women preachers claim to have had experiences with God's Spirit but not in quite the same way that Diane has. Carter Heyward, the irregularly ordained Episcopal priest, says she sometimes gets "whopped" by the Spirit and the result is an inner conviction that something she is doing is "so right and true."

"But when I talk about being 'Spirit-filled,' that doesn't relate to the charismatic movement," she explained. "I'm not a part of that. What I believe and what I mean by 'Spirit-filled' is probably what the charismatics mean, but they and I just don't talk from the same perspective. 'Spirit-filled' to me means being puffed up, filled, elated with the sense of God—something transcendent that's far beyond my control."

This spiritual dimension has been invaluable in sustaining Carter in her uphill fight for women's ordination in the Episcopal Church. She recalls that when she walked up to be ordained in Philadelphia in defiance of Episcopal tradition, she felt this "filling up" with the Spirit. "I was exuberant. Something very good was happening, but the power didn't come from inside me. I was totally out of control." In this tense and critical moment in her church career, Carter found that the validity of the events in which she was participating "was confirmed by the sense of the Spirit."

Carter says she also communicates regularly to God through prayer. "I pray conversationally sometimes, but it's a meditative kind of thing. Prayer to me is letting myself hang all out in an acute aware-ness of God. It takes the form usually of sitting or lying or walking or kneeling or whatever, and just trying to get honest with myself and with God about what's going on—wishes, prayers for other people and for myself. My prayers are not usually too topical because I find I ordi-narily don't know what to pray for. I pray that God's will be done. Prayers always bring answers, but I'm sure I often don't see the results of them. That's what faith is all about."

Carter's approach to God through prayer and her periodic sense of inner conviction that God is responding in some way are similar to the spiritual experiences of many other women pastors. A firm spiri-tual undergirding helps these women remain unwavering in the course they have set for themselves as ecclesiastical pioneers. Bonnie Jones-Goldstein, for example, says that God has spoken to her through dreams to give her confidence and certainty in her decision to be a Methodist minister.

"I had one dream about being ordained," she recalled. "When I was really ordained, it wasn't a spiritual experience I had connected with too well. But in the dream I did connect. It was very positive, like I'd *really* been ordained or 'called' this time. I sensed God was talking to me in a personal way through the dream.

"In my dream, the ordination service involved all women," she said, explaining that in her actual ordination the service was dominated by men. "I don't share this experience with a whole lot of people, by the way, because dreams are so foreign to most people's spiritual experi-ence. But they're important to me, and my faith is supported by them. A woman was ordaining me in the dream, and I received the answer to a lot of questions I'd been asking about my ministry."

She had posed these spiritual questions by writing them down in a diary, and when the answer came in the dream, she found she was "able to go beyond those basic questions and ask what I'd like to become as a minister. God is definitely a transcendent presence to me, and I don't believe I could produce these dreams by myself."

Diane Pierce, like Bonnie and many other women, has on occasion questioned her calling because of the many roadblocks that women pastors meet in pursuing their careers. But she has also found specific confirmation of her choice of profession in visions which can rival some of the accounts of St. Teresa. One of these visions was preceded by a walk she had in a wooded park one summer day with a friend who is a male pastor. Her companion suddenly stopped and said, "Do you feel the Lord here?"

"Yes," she replied, because she did "sort of feel a spiritual pocket on the path there."

Diane and the young man stood there quietly for a few moments, and listened to the birds chirping. "We had a sense the Lord was there, but we didn't see anything," she recalled. But when she returned home that night and was lying in bed reading, she had a vision that involved a "vivid experience of Christ." Here is the account of it that Diane recorded in her personal diary:

In that vision my friend and I were walking in the woods with my dogs, and we looked up at one point and saw the Lord standing off the side of the road ahead of us. He was bending over some bushes and didn't seem to notice us.

My friend and I looked at each other in amazement, and I finally managed to stammer, "Master."

He looked up and smiled and said, "Hello, my children, where are you going?"

We fell to our knees and my friend answered, "We're just out walking, master."

The Lord said, "Have you come to see me?" and my male companion answered, "Yes."

I was kneeling there wishing I could approach the Lord and kiss the wounds in his hands and feet, but I said nothing. He turned to me and said, "What do you want?"

I said, "May I come to you, Lord?"

He said, "To kiss my hands and feet?"

"Yes," I replied.

"If it would please you," he said.

I got up and started toward him. But I remembered I was in sin, so I stopped and said, "Forgive me, master, because I am unclean."

He smiled then, a transforming smile, and held out his hands and said, "You are clean."

So I knelt at his feet and kissed his wounds. He laid his hands on my head and said, "I don't want you ever again to doubt your calling. I love you. Receive my peace."

Then he called to my friend, who was still kneeling on the path with the two dogs and said, "Come, my son, and I will bless you also." So my friend got up and started toward us, but hesitated because he didn't know what to do with the dogs. The Lord said, "Let them go, they'll stay." And they just sat down on the path, wagging their tails.

My friend came and knelt before the Lord and the Lord said, "Receive my peace and accept my love."

We knelt there with heads bowed for several seconds and when we looked up, the Lord was gone.

Diane told her pastor friend about this vision the next day, and he asked, "Did you have a picture of where that took place?"

She thought back and, "sure enough, it was that exact spot on that path," where the two of them had sensed the presence of God the previous day. "We got kind of shaken up by that," Diane said. "It was a vision for both of us. It was a word for him and a word for me."

A skeptic might wonder how Diane and other women preachers are sure that these messages, revelations, and answers to prayer actually come from God. Do they use any test to determine whether their answers to prayer are valid? The most common pragmatic test seems to focus both on the intensity and the persistence of the sense of God's guidance.

Linda Harter, the Presbyterian minister who pastors two churches in upstate New York with her ordained husband, Bill, sometimes struggles hard against what she knows to be God's will. Almost like a modern-day Jacob who "wrestles" with the Lord, she especially resists giving sermons. "I like to preach once I'm up there, set to go, but I'd prefer to preach less than I do," she says, sighing. "Bill would like me to do more and I feel deep down I should do it, but the Lord and I have great arguments."

"Just like Moses, she doesn't want to do the job, doesn't want to carry the freight," her husband said with a grin.

"The inspiration just kind of has to work its way up through all kinds of layers of resistance," Linda explains. "I pray about it, but the creative process can be very agonizing. Once the hassle of Scripture and topic is settled, and an outline is formulated, the sermons flow very smoothly. God has his hand on us to shape us if we're willing to let him work. He has ways of guiding, prodding and changing. I'm stubborn by nature. But my better sermons are the ones I've had to struggle through."

In a similar vein, Diane Pierce sometimes tries to resist the divine guidance she receives. She senses that God tells her, "Relax and trust me," with great regularity, and occasionally it gets on her nerves. "I don't hear those words audibly, but I hear them inside me," she explains. "One time I was getting clothes out of the dryer and I was in a hurry and getting all tensed up. The Lord said, 'Will you please just relax?' "

Frustrated, she picked up some clothes and threw them across the room. "I wish you'd stop saying that!" she shouted.

Then she smiled in embarrassment and thought, "If anybody ever heard me say something like that, they'd think I was absolutely loony." At that point, her resistance melted away, and she felt the persistent, continuing sense of God's presence, which convinced her that the time had indeed come for her to relax.

Women preachers, then, have a variety of ways of tapping spiritual resources to gain strength and creativity as they carve new roles for themselves in the pastoral ministry. Some experience dramatic visions, revelations and dreams emanating from a transcendent God. Others rely more on a more subdued sense of inner conviction that God is guiding and sustaining. But whatever their theological predilections, these women recognize the importance of firm spiritual foundations to support them as they step into pulpits across the nation and take leading roles in American religious life.

In the earlier days of our nation, many communities, especially those on the frontier or in rural areas, built their public religious life around an individual called the "preacher-man." If a town was relatively prosperous, it might be able to support a full-time preacher. But more often than not, in the sparsely settled areas, the preacher-man roamed from one town and one farm to another with an old, battered Bible in his hand and the Word of God on his lips. As much as any other individual, these frontier preachers helped pioneer grass-roots religious traditions and set our style of morality and faith. A sort of countrified prophet and revival specialist, the preacher-man cited the Good Book as his primary spiritual authority. But actually, his real source of authority was his own spiritual experience and sense of mission, and the eloquence he could muster to convey his convictions.

There are similarities between today's female pastors and the tough, earthy country preachers of the past. The women, like their predecessors, confront a hostile environment, a frontier region. But their frontier is a frontier of the mind, of prejudice and male-oriented traditions. The women may also cite the Scriptures and church tradition as authority on matters of morality and theology. But the real source for their call, their conviction about their pastoral mission, always seems to center in an internal sense of spiritual truth and divine guidance. The Spirit in them is the ultimate authority and justification for their pastoral ministry. Arguments from Pauline theology or established church practice or any other source are either discarded or interpreted to fit into an overriding imperative that emanates from God and grasps their inner beings.

As they evaluate the profound challenges of their ministry, many of these female pastors cite the tribulations that confronted the Hebrew prophet Jeremiah as a precedent for their own hectic pastoral experiences. Jeremiah was a person who was called by God in much the way these women feel called.

"I appointed you a prophet to the nations," the Lord told Jeremiah. "Be not afraid of them, for I am with you to deliver you." And the Lord warned this prophet that the leaders and people of Judah would be against him: "They will fight against you; but they shall not prevail against you, for I am with you, says the Lord, to deliver you" (Jeremiah 1:19).

Today's women in the pulpit face many of the same tests, trials and criticisms that confronted Jeremiah as he attempted to persuade the Hebrews to reform their corrupt institutions and evil ways. The female pastors believe that one dimension of their calling is to convince male religious leaders and male-led congregations that women must be treated as equals whom God has designated for spiritual service. Churchmen and church institutions which resist this sense of divine mission are prime targets for prophetic wrath.

Jeremiah is sometimes known as the "weeping prophet" because he lived through a tragic period in Hebrew history, during the last days of the kingdom of Judah and the first part of the Babylonian captivity. By one tradition, he died as a martyr in Egypt, his prophecies unheeded by an exiled Hebrew people who had refused to accept his words as the Word of God. Many women pastors are also living through difficult times, facing discrimination and prejudice because of their sex. But while history has vindicated the words of Jeremiah, the validity of the unchartered and sometimes disruptive course of our female ministers still awaits final judgment.

The best advice in evaluating these daring, compassionate and sometimes strident pioneers may come from the Apostle Paul, a man who has often suffered abuse at the hands of modern churchwomen: "Do not quench the Spirit, do not despise prophesying, but test everything" (I Thessalonians 5:19–21). And as we test their spiritual authority and examine the fruits of their labors in the pulpit and parish, perhaps a few years hence we shall conclude that the trail-blazing women pastors of this era were indeed prophets who introduced a new wholeness into our religious life.